S0-CBD-515

Fish and their Sauces

micro wave

Madame Benoit

Encyclopedia of microwave cooking

micro wave

Fish and their sauces

Héritage plus

Front cover design: Philippe Bouvry, graphic artist, designer
Front cover and inside photography: Paul Casavant
Design and Research: Marie-Christine Payette
Dishes loaned by courtesy of: Eaton, downtown, Montreal
  and Le Curio, Montenach Mall, Beloeil.

Copyright © 1985 Les Éditions Héritage Inc.
All rights reserved

Legal Deposits: 4th quarter 1985
Bibliothèque nationale du Québec
National Library of Canada

ISBN : 2-7625-5807-7   Printed in Canada

LES ÉDITIONS HÉRITAGE INC.
300, Arran, Saint-Lambert, Québec J4R 1K5
(514) 672-6710

Table of Contents

Foreword

As fish occupies a most important place among the food essential to a properly balanced diet, we should cook it and eat it as often as we can. Nutritionists recommend that fish should be eaten as often as four times a week. The reasons are many. In the first place, fish is very low in that universal problem: "cholesterol fat". It is also one of the most digestible of high protein foods. Compared to red meat we are so fond of, fish contains only about a third of the calories per serving, and instead of saturated fat, fish has polyunsaturated fat. What's more, fish is relatively low in sodium, but high in iron, iodine and other beneficial minerals, and a plus is its excellent source of vitamins A and D.

Because fish lacks fiber, I always serve it with vegetables and grains such as rice, barley, etc.

I have enjoyed fish since my young days because my mother, who did not particularly like to cook, amazingly enough could always cook fish to perfection.

I have used many of her recipes to adapt fish cooking to microwave techniques. Not only were they successful, but the flavor and texture of the fish surpassed all of those which I so enjoyed, and believe me, it was not because I had cooked it but because the Microwave kept the fish texture and flavor at the peak of perfection.

Why was that? I asked myself. All fish is 60 to 80 per cent moisture. The juices must be retained during the cooking period, if the fish is to be tender and flavorful.

What other method of cooking can do this as easily as microwave cooking? This modern technology has increased comfort, ease of work, perfection in cooking, the possibility of retaining the full flavor of any food, the incredible reduction in hours of work, and the feasibility for many members of the family, even young ones, to cook their own meals when necessary, thus giving the working mother a freedom she has never known before. And the big plus, the quality in texture, color and flavor of all types of food cooked in the microwave oven.

I am often told: "I would not have the patience to change all my recipes". Microwave cooking doesn't entail learning a whole new method of cooking, but simply adapting to the microwave oven, and it is so easy with fish. First, make sure you know what type of fish you wish to cook: fat like salmon, delicate like sole, thick like haddock, etc. Fresh or frozen, whole, or thick or thin fillets. This will help you to determine the cooking period.

Remember that fish contains the same amount of protein as meat, but it is also important to be aware that it contains very little fat compared to meat. And as fat is a poor conductor of heat, this lack of it in fish means that heat penetrates much faster in fish than it does in meat.

The most important point is to be careful of the cooking time. Even when I say: "Cook 5 minutes at HIGH", do check after 3 minutes. Why? Because the thickness and the moisture of each type of fish varies, which can alter the cooking time by a minute or so, more or less. It is easy to know when fish is cooked, because the proteins become firm. They set in the sauce in the same way as the white of an egg. Another good rule is to cook the fish 5 minutes per inch of thickness (2.5 cm). If you have a fillet or a steak, place the piece of fish between two fingers to see how thick it is. Then cook accordingly. But if the fish is frozen, the cooking time will be double.

Do not salt fish before cooking because salt draws out the juices and makes it taste flat rather than enhancing its flavor. Salt when the fish is cooked.*

Be sure you know what type of fish you wish to cook, fat like salmon, delicate like Dover sole, thick like haddock, etc., because while fish contains the same amount of protein as meat, it is important to be aware that it also contains very little fat, as I have already explained.

* Some recipes call for salt due to a sauce or certain vegetables included in the recipe.

Introduction

In the course of time, many changes and modifications have taken place with regard to the preparation and cooking of food, table setting, and the time spent at such tasks. What a journey, going back to the time of the wood stove, which was still part of our daily life, even up to the years 1915 and 1920. Then, suddenly, important changes took place, gas and electricity for cooking, bringing about new kitchen equipment, new methods, savings in time, cleaning made easier, and not the least. . . white and elegant new stoves.

And now! A further gigantic step, which is changing and will continue to change many things... microwave ovens!

You buy a microwave oven, put it in the car, bring it home, place it on the kitchen counter, plug it in, and it's ready for use! And it's so easy for everyone to cook their favorite dishes in a microwave oven.

I, myself, started with the wood stove, and the memory still lingers on of those large slices of homemade bread toasted on top of the stove, and savored with fresh churned butter, homemade jam and café au lait with whole milk. What a delight! Of course, at that time, there was someone to rise at 5 a.m. to light the stove, and in the evening to rake over the ashes. There was a cook to churn the milk and make butter, and who spent innumerable summer hours making all that delicious jam.

Then followed the advent of the gas stove, with its coin-operated meter. If you forgot to feed in those 25¢ pieces, the gas was turned off! Still, it was an improvement over the wood stove. And one day the electric stove made an appearance. . . a miracle! We had seen nothing yet!

Modern technology has brought comfort, ease of work, perfection in cooking, the possibility of retaining the full flavor of food, the incredible reduction in hours of work, and the feasibility for each member of the family to cook his or her own meal, which gives the working mother a freedom she had never known before. This has been my experience: I cook more than ever before, yet my time spent in the kitchen has been reduced considerably. After thirteen years of cooking with microwave ovens, now I couldn't live without one. I have come to realize that you cannot know the true flavor of a vegetable or fish until you cook it in a microwave oven. And I can assure you that you need not learn a whole new cooking method, but simply learn to adapt your cooking to the microwave oven.

Many people have said to me: "I would not have the patience to change all my recipes", and so, I have decided to write this Encyclopedia of Microwave Cooking, so that you may realize how easy this method is once understood.

Microwave cooking is equally convenient for the small family with everyone working outside, as it is for the large family where larger servings are needed. All that's needed is knowing how to proceed.

The importance of knowing your oven

There are many models of microwave ovens, even of the same brand. It is therefore of utmost importance to become well acquainted with your oven, and to know and understand all its features.

What to do

- Once the oven is plugged in, place a bowl of water in it, close the door, and read the operation manual following every step as suggested.
  Example: Heat oven at HIGH for 2 minutes.

Look for Power Select HIGH and program, then look for the START setting; touch to put the oven on. You will then understand how this operation works.

Repeat this procedure for all types of operations, and very soon you will realize how easy it is, and you will understand how your own oven works.

Be Knowledgeable About Microwave Terms
There are many brands of microwave ovens on the market. That is why it is important to understand the language. Read and learn the following notes and microwave cooking will become clear and easy.

High or Full Power
This means a continuous cycle with maximum (100%) output, whatever your brand of oven.
The recipes in each volume of this encyclopedia were prepared for microwave ovens with wattage in the 650 - 700 range. If your oven has a lower output, increase the cooking time slightly according to the conversion chart.

All recipes in this book have been tested in a 650 and a 700-Watt microwave oven.
However, if you are using an oven with less wattage here is a comparative chart which will permit you to adjust the cooking time.

650-700W	500-600W	400-500W
15 seconds	18 seconds	21 seconds
30 seconds	36 seconds	42 seconds
45 seconds	54 seconds	1 minute
1 minute	1 min. 10 sec.	1 min. 25 sec.
2 minutes	2 min. 30 sec.	2 min. 45 sec.
3 minutes	3 min. 30 sec.	4 minutes
4 minutes	4 min. 45 sec.	5 min. 30 sec.
5 minutes	6 minutes	7 minutes
6 minutes	7 min. 15 sec.	8 min. 25 sec.
7 minutes	8 min. 25 sec.	9 min. 45 sec.
8 minutes	9 min. 30 sec.	11 minutes
9 minutes	10 min. 45 sec.	12 min. 30 sec.
10 minutes	12 minutes	14 minutes
15 minutes	18 minutes	20 minutes
20 minutes	24 minutes	27 minutes
25 minutes	30 minutes	34 minutes
30 minutes	36 minutes	41 minutes

This chart gives you an idea of the time needed for any food you cook in an oven with the above wattage.
However, it is always wise, regardless of wattage, to check the cooking when 2 minutes of the cooking period still remain. That's assuming, of course, that the cooking time indicated is over 2 minutes.

Let Stand
Many recipes read "Let stand x minutes after cooking". Since the microwave process of cooking is actually intense molecular vibration, food continues to cook even after the microwave energy is turned off.
In a way, the same happens when food is cooked in x time in an ordinary oven and we let it stand.
With microwaves the standing time lets the molecules come to rest. This is just like a bouncing ball that dribbles down to a gradual stopping point. It is often referred to as "aftercook".
When a recipe says "Let stand x minutes, stir and serve," that is exactly what is meant.

Rotate

If your oven has a turntable or a special system, such as Rotaflow, or the microwave oven over the stove which has a hidden turntable that does the same work as the rotating type, then you do not have to rotate the dish in which the food is cooking. Otherwise, give a quarter turn to the dish once or twice during the cooking period.

Microwave-proof Dishes or Utensils

All dishes and utensils suitable for microwave cooking (e.g.: Pyrex, Corning, Micro-Dur, Earthenware casseroles, etc.).

Elevate

This term is most often used for meats. It means placing the roast or chicken, etc., on a rack or an inverted saucer to allow cooking juices to drain off from under the meat.

After microwaving a roast, allow meat to cool slightly, still on a rack to allow surface air to cool it evenly.

Another example: when making muffins or cupcakes, cool for at least 10 minutes, on a rack, to allow air to cool the food evenly.

Variable Power

This describes the choice of power levels that allow you to prepare food in the microwave which normally would be over sensitive to continuous microwave activity. To easily understand this process, it is actually an "on and off" cycle timed for varying amounts of microwave energy, which means that this pulsating action effectively creates slower cooking activity, without your having to worry about it. If your recipe calls for 1/2 power, this equals MEDIUM-SLOW, which is like constant simmering.

When microwave cooking first began, ovens had only "Cook" and "Defrost" cycles. Some of you may still have these ovens, so remember that you effectively "simmer" on the Defrost cycle or whenever 1/2 power or MEDIUM is called for. For all other cooking, use the Cook cycle and add a few minutes to the cooking period called for in the recipe.

Temperature Probe

A thermometer-like, heat sensoring device to measure internal temperature of food during microwaving. Use only the "Probe" designed for your oven. It is perfect to cook a roast, by inserting the "Probe" in the meat, connecting it to the oven, then choosing the number referring to the cooking you wish to have; (e.g.: for a rare or well done roast, cook at the line printed on the oven time board and touch number indicated, then oven will start the cooking and at one point will give the degree of temperature needed to have the meat cooked according to your taste). You never have to worry how long it should take, since your oven will do it for you, and to perfection. Prepare the roast according to the recipe you are following.

Note : *Never use a conventional thermometer in the microwave oven.* There are many other ways to cook in the microwave, so always be ready to give serious attention to your oven manual, and you will soon find it is all very easy.

Degree of Moisture in Food

(1) The degree of moisture in food:
   the higher it is: faster and shorter cooking period. — e.g.: spinach;
   the lower it is: slower and longer cooking period. — e.g.: carrots.
(2) The quantity of liquid added to the food:
   the greater the quantity, the longer the cooking period will be.
(3) The density of produce:
   Porous = faster cooking: tomatoes, spinach, mushrooms, etc.
   More dense = longer cooking: peas, lentils, etc.
(4) Room temperature is the ideal temperature to start cooking:
   Warmer temperature = faster cooking with food at room temperature;
   Colder temperature = longer cooking with food taken from refrigerator or after thawing.
(5) The structure of the food:
   Smaller pieces = faster cooking: a small potato;
   Larger pieces = slower cooking: a large potato.
(6) Often foods are covered during the cooking period to prevent the natural moisture from evaporating because the water in these foods has been activated.
(7) The degree of sugar content determines the degree of heat produced:
   The more sugar, the more intense the heat and the shorter the cooking period: syrup, caramel, etc.
(8) The more fat in food, the faster it will cook.
(9) The arrangement of the food plays an important role:
   4 to 5 potatoes placed in a circle will cook faster than if they were simply placed in the oven.

(10) Degree of moisture - adding of water - density - thickness - structure - covers - amount of sugar - degree of fat - arrangement of food - appropriate accessories - are all key words relating your cooking to the factors of heat, weight and temperature.

How to cook food in the Microwave Oven

Microwaves are a form of high frequency radio wave similar to those used by a radio including AM, FM, and CB.
Electricity is converted into microwave energy by the magnetron tube, and microwaves are approximately four to six inches (10 to 15 cm) long with a diameter of about one-fourth inch (6mm). From the magnetron tube, microwave energy is transmitted to the oven cavity where it is: reflected, transmitted and absorbed.

Reflection

Microwaves are reflected by metal just as a ball is bounced off a wall. That is why the inside of the oven is metal covered with epoxy. A combination of stationary (interior walls) and rotating metal (turntable or stirrer fan) helps assure that the microwaves are well distributed within the oven cavity to produce even cooking.

Transmission

Microwaves pass through some materials such as paper, glass and plastic much like sunlight shining through a window. Because these substances do not absorb or reflect the microwave energy, they are ideal materials for microwave oven cooking containers.

Absorption

During heating, microwaves will be absorbed by food. They penetrate to a depth of about 3/4 to 1½ inches (2 to 4 cm). Microwave energy excites the molecules in the food (especially water, fat and sugar molecules), and causes them to vibrate at a rate of 2,450,000,000 times per second. This vibration causes friction, and heat is produced. If you vigorously rub your hands together, you will feel heat produced by friction. The internal cooking is then done by conduction. **The heat** which is produced by friction is conducted to the center of the food.

Foods also continue to cook by conduction during standing time, which keeps the cooked food warm for 4 to 10 minutes after cooking, and makes it possible to cook 3 to 4 dishes with only one oven, and to serve everything warm.

Example: If your menu calls for a roast, potatoes and green peas, cook the roast first. During its waiting period, cook the potatoes, they will remain warm from 20 to 30 minutes covered with a cloth, then the vegetable with the shortest cooking period.

The dessert may be cooked before the meat, or if it is to be served hot, cook it during the meal and let it stand in the oven. The oven goes off when the bell rings, and the food may be left inside until it is time to serve it.

Cooking equipment

Microwave cooking opens new possibilities in convenience and flexibility for cooking containers. There are new microwave accessories constantly being introduced, but do not feel you need to purchase all new equipment. You will be surprised at the numerous items you already have in your kitchen that are suitable for microwave cooking.

Glass, Ceramic and China

Most of these utensils are excellent for use in the microwave oven. Many manufacturers now identify microwave oven safe dishes. Heat resistant glassware, unless it has metallic trim or decoration, can most always be used. However, be careful about using delicate glassware since it may crack, not from microwave energy, but from the heat of the food.

Here are a few heat-resistant glass cookware items I find invaluable in microwave cookery. You probably have many of these items on your shelf already:
- glass measuring cups
- custard cups
- mixing bowls
- loaf dish
- covered casserole dishes
- oblong baking dish, non-metallic
- cake dishes, round or square, glass
- pie plate, plastic, glass or ceramic
- large bowls, 8 to 10 cups (2 to 2.5 L), with covers
- cake dishes, round, long, square, Pyrex, plastic, "Micro-Dur".

Browning Dish (Corning)

There are two sizes: 8 x 8 x 2 inches (21 x 21 x 5 cm) — 6 cups (1.5 L)
               9.5 x 9.5 x 2 inches (24 x 24 x 5 cm) — 10 cups (2.5 L)
There is also a Browning Grill: 8 x 8 inches (21 x 21 cm).

A Browning Dish has a special dielectric coating on the underside. The coating is activated by preheating (uncovered) the empty Browning Dish for no more than 7 minutes for the smaller one or 9 minutes for the larger one or for the grill in the Microwave.

Do not remove dish from oven after preheating, simply place in the preheated dish the steak, or whatever you wish to brown, pressing down on the food with a fork to obtain perfect contact with the bottom of the dish. If the recipe calls for oil or butter or other fat, it must be added after preheating the dish. Brown 5 to 7 minutes or according to recipe. You will be surprised how well browned the food will be. Turn it and let stand in the dish in the Microwave the time it took to brown the bottom part, without heat, as giving it more cooking time will only dry the food. It is then ready to serve.

A Browning Dish can be an extremely handy accessory with many uses: to brown steaks and chops, etc., stir-fry vegetables, cook omelets, reheat pizzas, grill sandwiches, and much more.

Do not limit these items to being browners only! They are just as useful as regular microwave cookware. Without preheating, the base will not get hot so can be used for microwaving vegetables, casseroles, desserts, fish, etc. The Browning Dish cover is used more frequently for this type of cooking.

Browning Dishes are for use in Microwaves only, and not in regular ovens (coating could be scratched by oven racks), or on range top as possible damage to special coating could result.

Do not use Probe with the Browning Dish.

Cooking bags

Cooking bags designed to withstand boiling, freezing or conventional heating are safe to use in the microwave oven. Make six small slits in the top of the bag to allow steam to escape. If you use twist-ties to close the bag, make sure the ends are completely rolled around the bag, not loose, as they could act as an antenna and cause arcing (blue sparks). It is better to use a piece of cotton string or a nylon tie, or a strip cut from the open end of the bag. DO NOT COOK FOOD IN BROWN OR WHITE PAPER BAGS.

Plastic wrap

Plastic wrap such as Saran Wrap™ and others can be used to cover dishes in most recipes. Over an extended heating time, some disfiguration of the wrap may occur. When using plastic wrap as a casserole dish cover, fold back a small section of plastic wrap from the edge of the dish to allow some steam to escape. When removing plastic wrap "covers", as well as any glass lid, be careful to remove it away from you to avoid steam burns. After heating, loosen plastic but let dish stand covered. Please note that it is not always necessary to cover all foods.

Food Covering for Sensor Cooking

When cooking by Sensor method an inch (2.5 cm) of water is needed in the bottom of the dish and the dish must be covered with plastic wrap. The Microwave-safe plastic dish "MICRO-DUR" does not need the plastic wrap as its cover keeps the steam inside the dish.

Aluminum foil

Aluminum foil can be used safely when certain guidelines are followed. Because it reflects microwave energy, foil can be used to advantage in some cases. Small pieces of foil are used to cover areas such as the tips of chicken wings, chicken legs, or roasts that cook more quickly than the rest. Foil is used in these cases to slow or stop the cooking process and prevent overcooking. The strips of foil placed on the edges of a roast or the ends of chicken legs can be removed halfway through the cooking period.

Food characteristics

Food characteristics which affect conventional cooking are more pronounced with microwave heating.

Size and quantity

Microwave cooking is faster than cooking with gas or electricity, therefore the size and quantity of food play an important role in cooking time.

Shape

Uniform sizes heat more evenly. To compensate for irregular shapes, place thin pieces toward the center of the dish and thicker pieces toward the edge of the dish.

Bone and fat

Both affect heating. Bones conduct heat and cause the meat next to it to be heated more quickly*. Large amounts of fat absorb microwave energy and meat next to these areas may overcook.

*See Aluminum foil paragraph.

Starting temperature

Room temperature foods take less time to heat than refrigerator or frozen foods.

Spacing

Individual foods, such as baked potatoes and hors d'oeuvres, will heat more evenly if placed in the oven equal distances apart. When possible, arrange foods in a circular pattern.
Similarly, when placing foods in a baking dish, arrange around the outside of dish, not lined up next to each other. Foods should NOT be stacked on top of each other.

Stirring

Stirring is often necessary during microwave cooking. Recipes advise as to frequency of stirring.

Example: *Always bring the cooked outside edges toward the center and the less cooked center portions toward the outside. Some foods should be turned in the container during heating.*

Standing time

Most foods will continue to cook by conduction after the microwave oven is turned off. In meat cookery, the internal temperature will rise 5°F to 15°F if allowed to stand, covered, for 10 to 20 minutes. Casseroles and vegetables need a shorter amount of standing time, but this standing time is necessary to allow foods to complete cooking in the center without overcooking on the edges.

Power Select Settings

Some microwave ovens are equipped with multiple Power Select settings: HIGH, MEDIUM-HIGH, MEDIUM, MEDIUM-LOW, DEFROST, LOW, WARM, and DELAY/STAND.
While most foods can be heated on HIGH (full power), certain types of foods, milk for example, will benefit from heating with a reduced amount of energy over a slightly longer time.
This variety of settings offers you complete flexibility in microwave cooking.

IMPORTANT

The following recipes were tested in 650 - 700 watt microwave ovens.

Lower-wattage ovens may necessitate some adjustment in timing. (See chart on page 10).

The recipes in general will serve 6 medium portions or 4 large portions.

Power Level Chart

Power	Output	Use
HIGH	100%..................... (700 watts)	Boil water Brown ground meat Cook fresh fruits and vegetables Cook fish Cook poultry (up to 3 lb [1.5 kg]) Heat beverages (not containing milk) Make candy Preheat Browning Dish (accessory)
MEDIUM-HIGH	90%..................... (650 watts)	Heat frozen foods (not containing eggs or cheese) Heat canned foods Reheat leftovers Warm baby food
MEDIUM	70%..................... (490 watts)	Bake cakes Cook meats Cook shellfish Prepare eggs and delicate food
MEDIUM-LOW	50%..................... (360 watts)	Bake muffins Cook custards Melt butter and chocolate Prepare rice
LOW	27%..................... (200 watts)	Less tender cuts of meat Simmer stews and soups Soften butter and cheese
WARM	10%..................... (70 watts)	Keep foods at serving temperature Rise yeast breads Soften ice cream
"Defrost"	35%..................... (245 watts)	All thawing, see Defrosting Charts
"Delay Stand"	0%..................... (0 watts)	Start heating at later time Program stand time after cooking

IMPI — International Microwave Power Institute — is an international institution governing microwave data throughout the world for kitchens, hospitals, etc.
IMPI have set the standards which have been adopted with regard to the designation of Power Settings for Microwave Ovens: HIGH, MEDIUM-HIGH, MEDIUM, MEDIUM-LOW, LOW, REHEAT, DEFROST, START, which must be observed everywhere in the world.

Halibut "À la Grecque"
(page 78)

It is to our advantage to study and make use of the innovative technologies in microwave ovens, as they always make it easier for us. Do make sure to read the instructions in your oven manual to learn about and understand the various cooking methods your oven has to offer and their use.

The following are some features which you need to acquaint yourself with in order to take full advantage of them.

Magnetic Turntable

Some ovens are equipped with an automatic magnetic turntable or a small fan in the top of the oven, or an invisible rotating system (whichever is featured in your Microwave, it will be explained in your instruction manual), then you do not have to rotate the dish.

If your Microwave has neither turntable, nor fan, nor invisible rotating system, then you will have to rotate the dish for even cooking as the Microwave may tend to focus more on a definite spot in the food, especially if there is fat in the meat, and remember that they are not always visible. What happens is that the fat parts cook more quickly because the reflection area is not altered, so, of course the cooking dish may be rotated.

Auto Sensor Cooking

The Auto Sensor is yet another wonder of Microwave cooking! The Microwave oven determines the cooking time. You wish to cook either a vegetable, meat, poultry, stew, etc., and are wondering what cooking time to allow. Relax.

If your Microwave features Auto Sensor Cooking it will be indicated on the oven panel with a COOK or INSTA-MATIC, etc. section, and your oven manual will give you instructions as to its use.

Numbers 1 to 7 or 8 are also shown on the panel, each one indicating the type of food for cooking, e.g. A7 Soft Vegetables (brussels sprouts, zucchini, etc.); A8 Hard Vegetables (carrots, etc.) Always refer to your oven manual for precise instructions.

There are two important points to remember when cooking by Auto Sensor (COOK). Whatever the food, a little water must always be added, from 1/4 to 1/3 cup (60 - 80 mL), depending on the quantity, and the dish must be well covered with either plastic wrap or a tight-fitting lid that will hold securely in place throughout the cooking period. There are some dishes, of various shapes and sizes, with a perfect lid for Auto Sensor Cooking which are available on the market. They are called "Micro-Dur".

- It is important that the oven door not be opened during the cooking period. The operation takes place in two stages.
- The selected number appears and remains in the display window until such time as the steam is detected by the humidity sensor, which is inside the oven. At this time a BEEP is heard and the cooking time appears in the display window.

A few hints for reheating food in the Microwave Oven

Like defrosting, reheating a wide variety of foods is a highly appreciated use of a microwave oven. It not only saves time, money and clean-up, but most foods reheat so well that there is little loss of taste. Leftovers take on that "just cooked" flavor which has never been possible when reheating by conventional methods. Many foods are actually better when reheated because they have had time to allow the flavors to blend.

Such foods as spaghetti sauce, lasagna, mashed potatoes, creams, stews are examples of foods whose flavor improves with reheating.

A plate of food

Arrange foods on a microwave-safe plate with thicker or denser portions towards the rim of the plate. Add gravy or butter where desired. Cover plate with waxed paper, reheat at MEDIUM-HIGH for 2 to 3 minutes, checking after 2 minutes.

To reheat by Sensor
Prepare plate in the same manner, cover completely with plastic wrap, and touch pad 1 of Sensor or any other as instructed in your microwave manual, that is, of course, if you have a Sensor pad on your oven. The oven does the work. You do not have to determine the time.

Casseroles
Stir well and add a small amount of liquid (water, milk, consommé, gravy, etc.), usually 1/4 cup (60 mL) is sufficient, cover with a glass lid or plastic wrap. Again if your oven has a Sensor or Insta-matic Cooking Heat, touch pad 1 or as directed in your microwave manual.

To reheat by time
Cover with waxed paper and heat at MEDIUM-HIGH for 2 to 6 minutes, stirring halfway through heating.

Weight defrost

Certain ovens have a choice of defrosting by weight or defrosting by time-defrost method. You can use your weight defrost method which is very accurate by first reading the directions given in your operation manual. Weight Defrost is based on the following automated cycle. Defrost Cycle for Meats and Poultry Pieces goes between 0.1 lb (approximately 1½ oz.) and 5.9 lb. By touching the weight and defrost pads of your oven control panel, the automatic count-up system will indicate in the display window the weight from 1 to 6 lb (0.5 to 3 kg) of such common meat and poultry items that are usually defrosted.
Again I would like to repeat, if your oven has this automatic weight defrost make sure you read the instructions given in your oven manual so it will be fully understood.

Method for Defrosting Fish in the Microwave at Defrost Cycle

- Make a slit in top of package with the tip of a knife. Open package at both ends. Place the package on an inverted plate covered with a paper towel, which allows hot air to circulate around fish and helps defrosting. Program the oven at DEFROST cycle and proceed as follows:
- Defrost for 2 minutes 15 seconds, let stand 3 minutes (there is no need to remove it from the oven).
- Turn, then defrost another minute and let stand 2 minutes.
- Turn and defrost for 2 minutes.
- Remove fish from package. It may still be slightly frozen in the center, which will not prevent you from cutting the fish in four equal parts or dividing it into fillets, to cook it as you wish.
- If your oven has a DEFROST BY WEIGHT, follow directions given in your oven Manual.

Another Method for Defrosting Fish

If your oven does not have a special Defrost button or a Defrost by Weight, here is the way to proceed: Place the frozen package (unless wrapped in foil, then it must be opened) on a double thickness of paper towel laid on the oven tray. Set oven at DEFROST or MEDIUM, turn package once during thawing time.
It usually takes a 1 pound (500 g) fish fillet 3 minutes to defrost sufficiently to allow you to separate fillets under cold water.
Always cook defrosted frozen fish shortly after defrosting. Use any of the methods given in this book to cook the fish.

Method for Defrosting Fish Sticks

If your oven has the DEFROST-COOK cycle, follow the instructions given in your oven manual. If you wish to defrost your fish sticks in the microwave oven, here's how to proceed. I also give you my favorite way to serve them.

1 lb (500 g) frozen fish sticks

Grated rind of half a lemon

1 tbsp. (15 mL) fresh minced dill (optional)

Place a rack in the bottom of a glass, plastic or ceramic dish, 12 x 8 inches (30 x 20 cm). Place the fish sticks on the rack, one next to the other, leaving a slight space between them. Do not cover. Cook 2 minutes at HIGH. Give the dish a quarter turn if your Microwave does not have a turntable. Cook again 2 minutes at HIGH. Remove from oven and let stand 5 minutes, cook 1 minute more at HIGH. The fish sticks will be completely thawed and very tasty. Serve with a sauce of your choice or sprinkle the fish sticks with lemon rind and dill.

Basting Fish

Contrary to meat, fish will be more tasty and moist if basted at least once during the cooking period. If there is a sauce surrounding the fish, use it to baste the fish.

Or use one of the following:

- 2 tablespoons (30 mL) hot water, 2 tablespoons (30 mL) butter;
- 2 tablespoons (30 mL) hot water, 4 tablespoons (60 mL) white wine;
- 1/4 cup (60 mL) hot water, juice of half a lemon;
- 1/3 cup (80 mL) hot tomato juice;
- 3 tablespoons (50 mL) sour cream or whipping cream.

Obviously each of these ingredients will produce a different flavor, as well as give a different texture to the fish. But any of these will give good results and enhance the flavor of the fish.

General Directions

Clean fish before starting the recipe. Arrange fish in a single layer; do not overlap edges. You can also roll each fillet into a little bundle, this is especially good for thin fish fillets. This applies to whichever way you are cooking the fish. Shrimp and scallops should always be placed in a single layer for cooking.

TO COOK BY TIME: Cover dish with plastic wrap or a cover. Cook on the power level and for the minimum time recommended in the chart.

- Make sure to stir or re-arrange shrimp and scallops halfway through cooking period.

TO COOK BY AUTO SENSOR OR "COMB." (Combination): Cover dish completely with plastic wrap. Cook on Auto Sensor Cycle COOK A8, or as directed in your oven Manual.*

- With shrimp or scallops, stir when cooking time appears in the display window or your oven.
- For fish and seafood dishes, let stand, covered, 5 minutes after cooking.

Test for doneness before adding extra heating time. When cooked, fish and seafood should be opaque in color and fish should flake when tested with a fork. If undercooked, return to oven and continue cooking 30 to 60 seconds more.

Study your oven Manual instructions carefully to clearly understand instructions given in the following chart.

Important

Before cooking a whole fish or a thick piece of fish, wash it in very cold salted water. Use 1/4 cup (60 mL) coarse salt to 6 to 8 cups cold water. Let stand a few minutes and remove from water. Wipe excess water with paper towel.

Cooking Fish and Seafood

Fish or Seafood	Amount	Power	Approx. cooking time (in minutes)
All Fish Fillets	1 lb (500 g)	HIGH	4 to 6
Fish Steaks	4 (6 oz ea.)	HIGH	6 to 8
Scallops	1 lb (500 g)	MEDIUM	6½ to 8½
Shrimp medium size (shelled and cleaned)	1 lb (500 g)	MEDIUM	4½ to 6½
Whole fish (stuffed or unstuffed)	1½ to 1¾ lb (750 g)	HIGH	9 to 11

Preparing and Cooking Frozen Fish and Seafood
FREEZE-COOK CYCLE

Fish or Seafood	Auto Sensor cycle FREEZE-COOK	Approx. cooking time (in minutes)	Special instructions
Fish Steaks 1 lb (500 g)	FROZ-COOK A8	20 to 21	Individually frozen. Add 1/4 cup (60 mL) water per pound (500 g)
Fish Fillets 1 lb (500 g)	FROZ-COOK A8	18 to 19	Individually frozen. Arrange in single layer
Whole Fish 1 lb (500 g)	FROZ-COOK A6	20 to 21	Arrange in single layer. Add 1/4 cup (60 mL) water per pound (500 g)
Frozen Lobster Tails 8 oz ea. (250 g)	FROZ-COOK A8	15 to 19	
Scallops 1 lb (500 g)	FROZ-COOK A8	21 to 22	Arrange in single layer
Shrimp (peeled or in shell) 1 lb (500 g)	FROZ-COOK A6	22	Arrange in single layer

Basic Methods

Water Poached Fish

Use this method for small whole fish or sliced larger fish. Season each slice of fish with a few drops of lemon juice and a dash of pepper.

Place fish slices or steaks one next to the other as they were before being cut. Wrap whole fish in a cloth (any white cloth will do).

Pour 2 cups (500 mL) of warm or cold water into a 4-cup (1 L) plastic or glass dish with cover. Heat 10 minutes at HIGH. Uncover, place the wrapped fish in the hot water. Cook 3 minutes per pound (500 g) at HIGH. Do not cook more than 3 pounds (1.5 kg) at a time. Let stand 5 minutes in water. Remove and refrigerate or serve with the sauce of your choice.

Fish Boiled in Milk

Cut the fish of your choice into individual portions. Soak 5 minutes in cold water to cover and add 1 tablespoon (15 mL) of coarse salt. Drain.

Pour 2 cups (500 mL) of milk into a 6-cup (1.5 L) dish. Cover and heat 2 minutes at HIGH.

Place the fish in the boiling milk, cover and cook at HIGH 4 minutes per pound (500 g).

Note: If you wish to use the milk, remove fish from dish with a perforated spoon. Cream together 2 tablespoons (30 mL) flour with 2 tablespoons (30 mL) butter. Add to hot milk. Stir well. Cook 2 minutes uncovered. Stir well; if sauce is not sufficiently thickened, cook one more minute or as needed.

Fish Poached in Court-Bouillon

Place in an 8-cup (2 L) dish, 6 cups (1.5 L) of water, 1 tablespoon (15 mL) of coarse salt, 1/2 cup (125 mL) of cider vinegar*, 1 large carrot sliced, a few sprigs of parsley, fresh or dry, 1 bay leaf, 1/4 tablespoon (3.75 mL) thyme, 1/2 tablespoon (7.5 mL) whole peppercorns, 2 onions cut in four. Cook at HIGH 15 minutes. Let stand 15 minutes.

Pass through a sieve, reserving liquid which is put back into the baking dish. Add the fish and cook at HIGH. Time according to weight and type of fish.

* The vinegar can be replaced by an equal amount of fresh lemon juice or a small unpeeled lemon, thinly sliced.

For Poaching thin Fish Fillets

This method is used when poaching thin fillets such as sole or other fish of similar type.

Place fillets one next to the other in a buttered glass dish. Pour on top 1/4 cup (60 mL) of cream or milk or water or white wine. Each liquid will give a different flavor.

Sprinkle pepper and nutmeg on top of fillets. Cover dish with plastic wrap. Cook 3 minutes at HIGH. Let stand 5 minutes, salt fish and serve with your favorite sauce.

How to Poach Fish to Serve it Cold

There are many ways to poach different types of fish. The following is a basic recipe. It comes in handy when time is short. It can also be used as an aromatic bouillon in which the fish may be refrigerated when it is to be served cold.

Flavor as for poaching fresh fish.* Bring to boil 1/2 cup (125 mL) of water per pound (500 g) of fish. Pour over the fish. Cover the dish with plastic wrap and poach 2 minutes per pound (500 g) at HIGH. Make one or two slits in the plastic wrap and let fish cool in its cooking water. Then, without removing the cover, place in the refrigerator for 6 to 12 hours.

To serve, remove the skin when necessary, the same as for salmon. Place the fish on an attractive platter and coat with a gelatine mayonnaise. (See Sauce chapter).

* Use:

4-5 peppercorns

1 tsp. (5 mL) coarse salt

1 bay leaf

1/4 tsp. (1 mL) thyme

2 unpeeled slices of lemon (optional)

Fish Fumet

A "fumet" is used to poach fish, but especially as the liquid used to make an "aspic" or gelatine coating on top of a poached fish. Is is also used to make a Velouté or Sabayon sauce to serve with fish. I always keep some in my freezer in 2-cup (500 mL) quantity.

2 lb (1 kg) fish heads, bones and trimmings*	**1/2 tsp. (2 mL) thyme**
1 large onion, sliced	**10 peppercorns**
1 leek, sliced (optional)	**6 cups (1.5 L) water**
1 celery stalk, diced	**1 tsp. (5 mL) coarse salt**
2 tbsp. (30 mL) celery leaves	**2 cups (500 mL) white wine**
1 bay leaf	

Place in a 12-cup (3 L) pan, the fish heads and the trimmings, the onion, leek, celery, celery leaves, bay leaf, thyme, peppercorns, water and salt. Cover. Cook 10 minutes at MEDIUM-HIGH. Remove the scum that rises to the surface with a perforated spoon. Add the wine, cover. Cook at MEDIUM-HIGH 10 minutes. Let stand 15 minutes. Strain through a sieve lined with a cloth; you will then have a clear liquid.

* It is easy to obtain fish trimmings from a fish shop.

Baked Small Fish in the Microwave

This method will give you a crusty fish on top and a poached fish inside. Mix in an 8-inch (20 cm) cake pan, 2 cups (500 mL) of milk, 1/2 teaspoon (2 mL) each of salt and dry mustard, 1 bay leaf, 1/2 teaspoon (2 mL) of thyme. Cut the chosen fish in individual portions. Roll in this mixture and marinate 2 to 3 hours at room temperature.

Remove fish from milk and roll into fine breadcrumbs until well coated. Butter a dish large enough in which to place your pieces of fish, one next to the other.

Pour the following mixture on top: 3 to 4 tablespoons (50 to 60 mL) each of melted butter and lemon juice, using a large spoon to pour some of the mixture onto each piece of coated fish.

Cook at HIGH 4 minutes per pound (500 g). Serve as soon as cooked.

Stuffed Fillets of Fish

Butter generously an 8 x 8-inch (20 x 20 cm) ceramic or glass dish. Cover bottom with fish fillets placed one next to the other. Cover with the following stuffing:

Stuffing: This is a basic recipe that can be varied to taste. Butter 4 slices of bread on both sides. Crust can be removed to taste. Dice the bread. Add 1 egg lightly beaten, 2 small pickles, diced, 1/2 teaspoon (2 mL) paprika, 1/4 teaspoon (1 mL) thyme, 4 tablespoons (60 mL) milk, salt and pepper to taste. Mix thoroughly and use to cover fillets.

Cover stuffing with another layer of fillets.

Melt 1 minute at HIGH, 3 tablespoons (50 mL) of margarine or butter per pound (500 g) of fish. Add 1 teaspoon (5 mL) Dijon mustard, 1/4 teaspoon (1 mL) curry powder and the grated rind of half a lemon. Stir well and pour evenly over the top of the stuffing and fillets. Cook 12 minutes at MEDIUM-HIGH.

Oriental Steamed Fish

Any kind of fish can be steamed -- whether served hot or cold it is equally good. This method is especially recommended for a low fat or reducing diet.

Place 1½ to 2 inches (5 cm) of water in an 8 or 10-inch (20-25 cm) square ceramic or glass dish with a good cover. Choose a rack where at least 2 pieces of fish can be placed, although 1 to 6 individual pieces can be steamed at one time.

Pour 1½ to 2 inches (5 cm) of hot water in bottom of dish — or just what is needed to come to the level of the rack.

Place the pieces of fish on a plate or small platter, dot each piece with butter and a few drops of fresh lemon or lime juice. Set the plate on the rack. Cover the dish. Steam at HIGH 3 minutes per fillet or steak. Add 1 minute for each additional piece of fish. When cooked, remove from oven. Leave cover on, let stand 10 minutes and serve.

Japanese Steamed Fish

Roasted sesame seeds mixed with fresh ginger give a delicate and interesting flavor to fish fillets or smelts poached in this manner.

2 to 3 tbsp. (30 - 50 mL) sesame seeds

1 tsp. (5 mL) vegetable oil

1/4 cup (60 mL) Sake, water or white wine

1 tsp. (5 mL) fresh ginger root, grated

1/2 tsp. (2 mL) salt

2 lb (1 kg) fish of your choice

Sauce:

3 tsp. (15 mL) vegetable oil

1/4 cup (60 mL) soy sauce
   (Kikkoman if available)

1/4 tsp. (1 mL) fresh ground pepper

The roasted sesame seeds

1/2 cup (125 mL) green onions, minced

Place the sesame seeds and the 1 teaspoon (5 mL) vegetable oil in a small glass bowl. Brown 1 or 2 minutes at HIGH, stirring 3 times. When the sesame seeds are golden brown, set aside. Choosing a dish large enough to contain all the ingredients, pour into it the Sake, water or white wine, ginger root and salt. Cover and cook 5 minutes at MEDIUM to bring out the delicate ginger flavor. Add the fish to the hot liquid, basting it 3 or 4 times. Cover and cook 5 to 7 minutes at MEDIUM-HIGH, depending on type of fish used. Check doneness with a fork. The fish is cooked when it flakes. Let stand, covered, while you prepare the sauce.

The sauce: Mix together in a bowl, the vegetable oil, soy sauce, pepper and sesame seeds. Heat 40 seconds at HIGH. Pour over the cooked fish and sprinkle with minced green onions. Serve.

Fish Fillets "Bonne Femme"

Fresh or frozen fillets of a fish of your choice can be prepared with this classic of the French cuisine.

**1 to 2 lb (500 g to 1 kg) fish fillets
of your choice**

1 tsp. (5 mL) salt

1/4 tsp. (1 mL) pepper

3 tbsp. (50 mL) butter

2 garlic cloves, chopped fine

1 medium onion, cut in slivers

3 green onions, chopped

1/2 lb (250 g) fresh mushrooms, cut in four

1/2 cup (125 mL) dry cider or white wine

1/4 cup (60 mL) whipping cream

Roll the fillets in absorbent paper to remove excess moisture. Sprinkle with pepper and only 1/4 teaspoon (1 mL) of salt.

Preheat a browning dish (Corning) 5 minutes. Add the following into the hot dish, without removing from oven: butter, garlic, onion, green onions and half the mushrooms. Stir well. Add the remaining salt, stir. Cook at HIGH 2 minutes. Stir well.

Place the fillets rolled or left whole over the vegetables. Sprinkle remaining mushrooms on top. Pour the cider or wine over all. Cover pan with waxed paper and cook 4 to 5 minutes at HIGH. Let stand 3 minutes. Gently remove the fish to a hot platter with a perforated spoon. Also with the spoon, drain out most of the mushrooms and sprinkle on top and around the fish.

Cook the sauce 5 to 7 minutes at HIGH, or until reduced by half. Whip the cream and fold into the hot gravy while beating with a whisk.

Pour over fish and serve.

Butter Poached Fish Fillets

Easy and quick to make. Super when using fresh fillets of sole. Haddock, or cod are equally good, only the cooking period varies. The simplicity of the sauce makes it even better. Just dill or parsley mixed with lemon or lime juice. The fresh dill or parsley each give a different flavor.

2 lb (1 kg) fish fillets of your choice

1/3 cup (80 mL) butter

Salt and pepper to taste

Grated rind of 1 lemon

**1 tbsp. (15 mL) fresh dill, chopped or
1/4 cup (60 mL) fresh parsley, minced**

Place fish in a dish, cover with very cold water and add 2 tablespoons (30 mL) coarse salt. Let stand 30 minutes to 2 hours. This treatment prevents the fish from drying during the cooking period and accentuates its flavor. Remove the fish from water and dry thoroughly with paper towel.

Preheat a browning dish (Corning) 6 minutes at HIGH. Butter each fillet on one side. Without removing dish from the oven, place fish in it, buttered side down. Cook 2 to 3 minutes at MEDIUM-HIGH. Turn fillets, taking care not to break them. Cook 1 minute at HIGH. Remove fish to a hot dish, sprinkle with salt and pepper, lemon juice, dill or parsley, and to taste, some melted butter.

Fish Fillets or Slices Browned in Butter

You can make nice brown fish fillets or slices in the Microwave, using a browning dish (Corning).

1 lb (500 g) fish fillets or slices

1 egg white

2 tbsp. (30 mL) cold water or lemon juice

1 cup (250 mL) fine breadcrumbs

1 tsp. (5 mL) paprika

2 tbsp. (30 mL) butter, margarine or vegetable oil

Cut fillets into individual portions. In a small bowl, put the egg white slightly beaten with the cold water or lemon juice. Place breadcrumbs and paprika on a piece of waxed paper.
Melt butter or margarine 1 minute at HIGH.
Roll each fish piece in the egg white mixture, and then, in breadcrumbs.
Place the fish pieces on waxed paper and pour some of the chosen fat on one side of each piece.
Preheat a browning dish 5 minutes at HIGH. Without taking the dish out of the oven, put the fish pieces in it, buttered-side down. Press each piece with a fork. Cook 5 to 6 minutes at MEDIUM. Turn each piece with a spatula. Let stand 10 minutes in the oven or outside, covering dish with a cloth.
The top will be brown and crusty and the pieces well cooked.

Chinese Fish Fillets

2 tbsp. (30 mL) soy sauce

Grated rind of one lemon

1 tbsp. (15 mL) lemon juice

1 tbsp. (15 mL) ketchup

1 garlic clove, minced

1 tbsp. (15 mL) fresh ginger root, grated

1 lb (500 g) fish fillets of your choice, fresh or frozen

Mix together in an 8 x 8-inch (20 x 20 cm) glass dish the soy sauce, lemon juice and rind, ketchup, garlic and ginger. Cut the fish into individual pieces and set in the dish, rolling them around in the sauce.
Cover with waxed paper. Cook 5 to 6 minutes at HIGH, until the fish flakes easily. Let stand 5 minutes, covered. To serve, baste with the sauce in the dish.

Fillets "A l'Anglaise"

The easiest way to cook fish, but so tasty. Use fresh fish or thaw out frozen fillets.

1 lb (500 g) fillets of your choice
Juice and rind of 1 lemon

3 tbsp. (50 mL) melted butter or margarine
1/2 tsp. (2 mL) paprika

Cut fillets into individual pieces. Roll each piece in the lemon juice and rind mixed together.
Place in a single layer in an 8 x 8-inch (20 x 20 cm) glass dish or a 9-inch (22.5 cm) pie plate. Brush each fillet with melted butter or margarine. Sprinkle with paprika. Cover dish with waxed paper and cook 4 to 6 minutes at HIGH, depending on type of fish. Do not turn. Let stand 5 minutes. Serve with butter remaining in baking dish. Salt and pepper.

Baked Fish Fillets in Microwave-Convection Oven

Fish cooked by this method will have a nice brown color and will be moist and tender. Excellent method to cook salmon steaks, fresh thick fillets of cod or halibut or turbot.
- Brush each piece of the chosen fish with butter or oil or soft bacon fat, then roll in fine breadcrumbs. Place pieces of fish one next to the other, on a low heat-proof glass or ceramic dish. Do not overlap.
- Place low rack on turntable in your oven, if your model has one. Preheat microwave-convection oven 450°F. (230°C) (See your oven manual for instructions). When oven reaches set temperature, place fish dish on rack in preheated oven. Set oven again at 450°F. (230°C), cook 3 minutes per 3 pieces of fish. Time will vary slightly depending on the type of fish. Check cooking before removing from oven. Serve with a sauce of your choice.

Fish Fillets "Meunière"

A classic method of French cuisine to brown fish fillets. And believe me, a well-browned fish steak or fillet can be cooked with success in the Microwave.

It is important to note that fish, with its 60 to 80% moisture content and approximately 18% of albuminoid, must like eggs cook in a minimum of time, so as to retain the natural juices of a mild-flavor fish.

Use olive or vegetable oil in preference to butter which burns easily and gives the fish a milky taste.

1 egg white	**1 lb (500 g) thin fish steaks or fillets**
2 tbsp. (30 mL) cold water	**2 tbsp. (30 mL) vegetable oil**
2 tbsp. (30 mL) flour	**2 tbsp. (30 mL) butter**
1 tbsp. (15 mL) cornstarch	**1 tsp. (5 mL) capers or small gherkins, diced**
Salt and pepper to taste	

Mix together the egg white and the water in a deep plate.
Mix together the flour, cornstarch, salt and pepper on a piece of waxed paper.
Roll each piece of fish in the egg white mixture, then in the flour. Preheat a browning dish (Corning) 6 minutes at HIGH. Add the oil without removing the dish from the oven, place the fish pieces in it one next to the other, and press them down with a fork for perfect contact between the dish and the fish. Brown 6 minutes at HIGH. Turn carefully and let stand 6 more minutes in the oven, without heat. Serve on a hot plate, browned-side up.

Sole Fillets "En Cocotte"
(page 38)

Sole

Sole Embassy

In England, it is a super spring specialty, when asparagus and Dover sole are at their best. One of my favorite light lunches. Any type of sole can replace the Dover. Serve with fine noodles mixed with parsley and butter, to taste.

1 lb (500 g) fresh asparagus	3 tbsp. (50 mL) butter
Salt and pepper to taste	2 tbsp. (30 mL) lemon juice
Grated rind of half a lemon	2 green onions, minced
1 lb (500 g) sole fillets	1 tsp. (5 mL) Dijon mustard

Clean asparagus and cut into 3-inch (7.5 cm) lengths. Place in dish, add 1/4 cup (60 mL) water, a pinch of sugar. Cover and cook 5 minutes at HIGH. Drain. Stir with salt, pepper to taste and lemon rind. Divide equally over each fillet. Roll up and secure with wooden picks, or tie with soft string. Place the fish rolls side by side in a thickly buttered baking dish. Melt the 3 tablespoons (50 mL) butter 1 minute at HIGH. Add the green onions, lemon juice and the Dijon mustard. Heat 40 seconds at HIGH. Pour mixture over fish. Cover with waxed paper or a cover. Cook 6 minutes at MEDIUM-HIGH. Let stand 3 minutes and serve.

Sole Dugléré

Another great of the French cuisine. When the first fresh tomatoes appear in my garden, it has become a yearly delight to eat a "Dugléré".

1 lb (500 g) sole fillets	1 tbsp. (15 mL) butter
2 tomatoes, peeled and diced	2 tbsp. (30 mL) flour
1 tsp. (5 mL) sugar	1/2 cup (125 mL) white wine or white vermouth
1 medium-sized onion, diced	
1 garlic clove, chopped fine	Salt and pepper
1 tbsp. (15 mL) chopped parsley	

Place in a glass or ceramic dish, the tomatoes, sugar, onion and garlic. Mix well. Heat 2 minutes at HIGH.
Stir well, add the parsley. Place the fillets of sole on top of this mixture. Salt and pepper. Cover with waxed paper or plastic wrap. Cook 6 minutes at HIGH. Let stand 4 minutes.
Remove the fillets to a hot platter. Mix the butter and flour together and stir into the tomatoes. Mix well. Add the white wine or vermouth. Cook 4 minutes at HIGH, stirring well after 2 minutes. When sauce is creamy and piping hot, pour over the fish and serve.

Sole Amandine

One of the most popular of all fish dishes, from the classic French cuisine. Quick and easy to prepare with the microwave technique.

1 - 1½ lb (500 - 750 g) sole fillets	*Topping :*
2 tbsp. (30 mL) butter	2 tbsp. (30 mL) butter
1 tbsp. (15 mL) cornstarch	3 tbsp. (50 mL) thinly sliced almonds
Juice and rind of 1 lemon	
Pepper and paprika	

Place the first 2 tablespoons (30 mL) butter in a 12 x 8 inch (30 x 20 cm) glass or ceramic dish. Melt butter 1 minute at HIGH. Add the cornstarch, mix thoroughly. Add the lemon juice and rind. Stir to mix. Roll each fillet in this mixture. Roll each fillet into a round roll. Place one next to the other in the baking dish.

Sprinkle with the pepper and paprika. Cover dish with a piece of waxed paper or a cover. Cook 6 minutes at HIGH. Let stand 3 minutes. Salt to taste.

Place the butter and almonds in a small bowl. Brown 2 minutes at HIGH. Stir well; if the almonds are not sufficiently browned cook another 30 seconds, stir. This operation can be repeated a third time. However, stir often as the almonds can brown quite fast. They should be golden brown. Pour over hot fish and serve.

Italian Baked Sole Fillets

Fresh or frozen sole can be used for this dish. Defrost fish before cooking. Serve with creamed spinach, mixed with small noodle shells.

1 lb (500 g) frozen or fresh sole fillets

1 cup (250 mL) commercial sour cream

1/2 cup (125 mL) chopped green onions

1/2 tsp. (2 mL) salt

1/4 tsp. (1 mL) pepper

1 tsp. (5 mL) chopped basil

1/2 cup (125 mL) grated Parmesan or strong cheddar cheese

Paprika

To thaw fish see Index. Place either fresh or thawed frozen sole in a heavily buttered dish of 8 x 12 inches (20 x 30 cm). Combine remaining ingredients and spread evenly over the fish. Sprinkle the whole with paprika. Cover with plastic wrap, cook at MEDIUM 12 to 14 minutes for frozen fillets, and 6 minutes for fresh fillets. Let stand 5 minutes before serving. To cook by Sensor or "Comb." see time indicated for fresh fillets in your oven manual.

Sole "Vin Blanc"

In France, dry white Chablis is used to prepare this dish, and it is usually referred to as "Sole Chablis". However, any white wine can be used.

1 lb (500 g) fresh sole fillets

3 tbsp. (50 mL) butter

4 green onions, minced

1 cup (250 mL) dry white wine

4 tbsp. (60 mL) flour

3/4 cup (180 mL) cream

Juice of half a lemon

Salt and pepper

Stretch out each fillet on paper towel and pat dry.
In an oblong baking dish, melt 1 tablespoon (15 mL) of the butter, 1 minute at HIGH. Add the green onions, stir well, cook 1 minute at HIGH. Remove from baking dish and place rolled fillets in dish. Spread softened green onions on top. Pour wine over the fillets, cover dish with waxed paper or cover. Cook 5 minutes at MEDIUM-HIGH. Let stand 10 minutes, then remove fillets with a perforated spoon to a hot platter.
Place baking dish in microwave, cook uncovered 5 minutes at HIGH. Blend remaining butter with the flour. Add the cream and the lemon juice. Do not mix, simply pour the whole in the wine remaining from the fish. Stir well and cook 3 minutes at HIGH. Stir once during the cooking period. When smooth and creamy, salt and pepper to taste. Cook another 30 seconds, pour over the fish.

Sole Bercy

This one tops my list of favorites for its simplicity. The different possible combinations of ingredients give each variation of this dish a special finish.

6 green onions or 4 French shallots*

1/4 cup (60 mL) chopped fresh parsley or dill

1/4 cup (60 mL) white wine or dry white vermouth

1/4 cup (60 mL) fish fumet or clam juice

1½ to 2 lb (750 g to 1 kg) fillets of sole**

Juice of 1/2 lemon

3 tbsp. (50 mL) unsalted or salted butter, melted

1 tsp. (5 mL) cornstarch

Sprinkle the finely chopped green onions or French shallots, and the parsley or dill, over a generously buttered 8 x 12-inch (20 x 30.5 cm) glass or ceramic dish. Pour in the white wine or dry white vermouth, the fish fumet or clam juice. Lightly pepper the inside of each fillet, roll and set over ingredients in baking dish. Sprinkle with the lemon juice and the melted butter.
Cover dish with waxed paper. Cook at HIGH 6 minutes per pound (500 g) of fish, basting once during cooking period.
Remove fish to a platter, keep warm. Add the cornstarch to liquid in the pan. Stir until thoroughly mixed, salt and pepper to taste. Cook at HIGH 2 to 3 minutes or until creamy. Pour over the fish. To taste, surround with small boiled potatoes drained and rolled in finely chopped parsley.

 * French shallots have more flavor than green onions, but are sometimes hard to find and definitely more expensive; it's your choice.
** The fillets of sole can be replaced by haddock or halibut steak. Both will take 3 minutes more cooking time than fillets of sole.

Sole Fillets "En Cocotte" (photo page 32-33)

Very elegant luncheon dish or dinner "entrée". Easy to prepare and cook. It can be prepared in the lovely English egg cups with their cover, or in earthenware ramequins.

6 small fresh sole fillets

3 tbsp. (50 mL) butter

Juice of 1 lemon

1/4 tsp. (1 mL) of curry powder

1 tsp. (5 mL) of brandy or scotch

1/4 cup (60 mL) finely minced fresh mushrooms

salt and pepper to taste

Minced parsley or chives to garnish

Roll into individual portions. Place each portion in an English egg cup or ramequin.
Melt the butter 1 minute at HIGH, add the lemon juice, curry, scotch or brandy and mushrooms. Stir well. Divide equally over each cup of fish. Cover with plastic wrap. Place in a circle in the Microwave and cook 6 to 8 minutes at HIGH, or until fish is tender.
Very nice garnished with watercress, or with minced parsley or chives.

Sole in "Sauce Rosée"

The combination of white wine, mushrooms and tomatoes, gives a creamy sauce which cooks with the fish.

1 lb (500 g) sole fillets
Freshly ground pepper and salt to taste
1/4 cup (60 mL) finely minced parsley
1 cup (250 mL) finely chopped peeled tomatoes
1/2 tsp. (2 mL) sugar

1 cup (250 mL) sliced mushrooms
1/4 cup (60 mL) dry white wine or white Vermouth
1/2 cup (125 mL) light or heavy cream
3 tbsp. (50 mL) cornstarch or flour

Salt and pepper each fillet, sprinkle each one with some of the fresh parsley, roll and place in an 8 x 12-inch (20 x 30 cm) glass or ceramic dish.
Peel, seed and chop tomatoes and sprinkle evenly over the fish. Sprinkle sugar on top. Spread mushrooms evenly over the tomatoes. Mix together the wine, the cream and the cornstarch or flour. Pour over the fish. Cover with plastic wrap or a cover. Cook at MEDIUM-HIGH, 9 minutes, depending on thickness of fillets. Remove fish to a hot platter. Stir sauce thoroughly, cook at HIGH, 2 minutes. Stir well. The sauce should be creamy. It is sometimes necessary to cook it another 30 seconds to 1 minute, depending on the moisture in the fish. When creamy and hot, pour over the fish. Serve.

Sole Fillets Stuffed with Shrimp

The sole in this recipe can be replaced with a white fish steak of your choice or haddock fillets. Sole cooks faster than any other fish, so when using another type, it is well to remember to check the cooking every 2 minutes.

Filling :
1 tbsp. (15 mL) butter
2 tbsp. (30 mL) flour
1/2 cup (125 mL) milk or cream
1 cup (250 mL) peeled and diced shrimps
1/2 cup (125 mL) sliced mushrooms

6 fillets of sole
1/4 cup (60 mL) butter
1/2 cup (125 mL) fresh white breadcrumbs
1/2 tsp. (2 mL) paprika (optional)

Prepare filling by melting the butter 1 minute at HIGH, stir in the flour; add the milk or cream, salt and pepper to taste. Stir well. Cook 2 minutes at HIGH. Stir until creamy. Add the mushrooms and the shrimps. Taste for salt and pepper. Cook 1 minute at HIGH. Stir well.
Cover the bottom of a dish with half the fillets, pour the shrimp mixture on top. Cover mixture with the rest of the fillets. Mix the breadcrumbs with the melted butter and the paprika, scatter over the fillets. Cook 10 minutes at HIGH.
To taste, garnish with little bunches of watercress before serving.

Salmon

Poached Salmon

I like to serve poached salmon hot with an egg sauce or cold with a sour cream cucumber sauce; you will find both sauces in the Sauce chapter.

8 cups (2 L) water

Juice of 1 lemon

2 carrots, peeled and sliced

12 peppercorns

1 tbsp. (15 mL) coarse salt

6 to 10 parsley sprigs or
   1 tbsp. (15 mL) dried parsley

1 bay leaf

3 to 4 lb (1.5 to 2 kg) fresh salmon,
   in one piece

Choose a dish large enough to hold the salmon. Place all the ingredients in the dish except the salmon. Cover and cook at HIGH 15 minutes. Wrap the salmon in a wet J-cloth, sew up in a neat bundle and place in the boiling water. Pour water on top of fish with a soup ladle, 4 to 5 times. Cover dish and cook at MEDIUM-HIGH, 5 minutes per pound (500 g). Let stand 10 minutes.
Remove fish from water with two forks. Set on a plate.
To serve hot, unwrap and set on a dish. Top with finely chopped fresh parsley or dill and melted butter to taste — or use a sauce of your choice.*
To serve cold, do not unwrap, refrigerate 6 to 12 hours. Remove cloth and garnish to taste. Serve with a bowl of cold sauce of your choice.*

* See Sauce chapter.

English Poached Salmon

The perfect cold buffet fish.

A 3 to 4-lb (1.5 to 2 kg) piece of salmon,
   cut from the center

2 cups (500 mL) milk

2 cups (500 mL) water

1 tbsp. (15 mL) coarse salt

2 bay leaves

1/4 cup (60 mL) coarsely chopped parsley

1/2 tsp. (2 mL) basil

1/4 tsp. (1 mL) dill seeds

1 cup (250 mL) mayonnaise

1 peeled lemon cut into thin slices

2 hard-cooked eggs

2 carrots, finely shredded

Wrap and sew the piece of salmon in a J-cloth, as for Poached Salmon. Place in an 8-cup (2 L) bowl, the milk, water, salt, bay leaves, chopped parsley, basil and dill. Cover and cook at HIGH 15 minutes. Add the salmon, pour some of the hot liquid on top. Cover and cook at MEDIUM-HIGH 5 minutes per pound (500 g). Let stand 10 minutes. Cool 1 hour at room temperature. Do not unwrap, refrigerate overnight.
To serve, unwrap, remove the skin, set on a nice plate. Spread the mayonnaise all over the fish. On top, make a long line of overlapping slices of lemon. Grate the hard-cooked eggs and sprinkle over the whole fish.
Place the shredded carrots all around the fish, to form a sort of crown.
Set on a bed of crisp lettuce leaves.

Poached Salmon "À la Française"

In France, they prefer to use salmon steak for this dish. When I cannot get salmon, I replace it with halibut or fresh cod.
It is served cold with the classic "Sauce Verte".

1 tbsp. (15 mL) olive or vegetable oil

4 to 6 salmon steaks of your choice

Grated rind of 1/2 a lemon

Juice of 1 lemon

6 peppercorns, crushed

1 medium-sized onion, peeled and cut in 4

1 tbsp. (15 mL) coarse salt

Spread the oil in the bottom of a 12-inch (30 cm) square dish. Place the fish steaks one next to the other, not overlapping. Add the lemon juice and rind. Sprinkle the peppercorns and onion on top and add enough hot water, to just come to the top of the fish. Sprinkle the coarse salt in the water, around the fish. Cover and poach fish at HIGH 2 minutes per piece of fish. Let stand 10 minutes. Uncover and let the fish cool in its water.
Then remove each piece with a perforated spoon and remove the skin if necessary. Arrange on a serving plate.
Completely cover top of fish with "French Sauce Verte". (See Sauce chapter)
Can be refrigerated 6 to 8 hours.

Boiled Salmon at its Best

To my taste, the best way to cook fresh salmon in order to retain its delicate flavor is by boiling or steaming. The following recipe has remained one of my favorites for years. I have now adapted it to microwave cooking and I believe I could no longer return to the old method. And remember, salmon is at its best in the spring.

4 cups (1 L) hot water

2 bay leaves

1 tbsp. (15 mL) coarse salt

1 tsp. (5 mL) paprika

1 tbsp. (15 mL) marinating spices*

1/2 a large lemon, chopped

A 3 - 4-lb (1.5 - 2 kg) piece of fresh salmon

Place all the ingredients except the salmon in a large 12-cup (3 L) dish. Cover and cook 15 minutes at HIGH. In the meantime, wrap the salmon in a cheese-cloth or a piece of cotton. Sew it up to wrap tightly. When the bouillon is hot, place the fish in it. Cover and cook at HIGH 5 minutes per pound (500 g). Remove from Microwave and leave uncovered 20 minutes. Unwrap the fish when ready to serve and place it on a serving dish, remove the skin and backbone.
To serve it cold, let salmon cool in cooking water for 1 hour at room temperature, then refrigerate. It will keep perfectly for 3 days. To serve, unwrap, remove skin and bones. Serve the salmon hot with a Hollandaise, Bercy or Egg Sauce. Serve it cold with watercress mayonnaise or any mayonnaise of your choice.

* Commercial marinating spices are sold at the herb and spice counter in food stores.

My Mother's Curried Salmon

In the Spring, whenever my mother was able to have a nice piece of fresh salmon, she cooked it in the following manner.

2½ cups (625 mL) white wine, water,
   or half and half

2 tsp. (10 mL) salt

2 bay leaves

1 cup (250 mL) long grain rice

2 tbsp. (30 mL) butter

1 tsp. (5 mL) curry powder

2 lb (1 kg) fresh salmon

3 tbsp. (50 mL) butter

3 tbsp. (50 mL) flour

1 cup (250 mL) milk

1/2 cup (125 mL) light cream

3 egg yolks, lightly beaten

Salt and pepper to taste

Pour into a 12-cup (3 L) dish the white wine or the water or half and half. Cover and bring to boil 4 minutes at HIGH. Add the salt, bay leaves and rice. Stir well. Cover and cook at MEDIUM-HIGH 15 to 18 minutes. Remove from Microwave, stir and let stand covered 10 minutes.

Melt the 2 tablespoons (30 mL) butter 2 minutes at HIGH. Add the curry and stir to mix thoroughly. Leave the fish in one piece or cut into 4 thick steaks. Roll each steak or the whole piece of fish in the hot curried butter. Cover and cook at MEDIUM-HIGH 6 to 8 minutes, or until the fish flakes. Set aside and keep warm.

Melt the 3 tablespoons (50 mL) butter in a bowl or measuring cup 1 minute at HIGH. Add the flour, stir. Add the milk and cream and cook 4 to 5 minutes at HIGH, stirring twice. Beat the egg yolks, mix in 1/2 cup (125 mL) of the hot sauce, then add the remaining hot sauce. Beat with a whisk. Cook 2 minutes at MEDIUM, stirring once. Salt and pepper to taste.

Make a rice nest on a hot plate. Remove fish from cooking dish with a perforated spoon and place it in the middle of the cooked rice. Pour the hot sauce over it. If necessary, reheat 2 minutes at MEDIUM and serve.

Nova Scotia Spicy Salmon

At the beginning of Spring I prefer fresh salmon, especially when it comes from Gaspé, and then the one from Nova Scotia. By cooking it in court-bouillon it will keep refrigerated for 2 or 3 days. Serve it cold with hot boiled potatoes (cooked in the Microwave, of course) rolled in fresh parsley, and a small bowl of mayonnaise stirred with an equal amount of Dijon mustard or horseradish.

1/2 cup (125 mL) cider vinegar

2 cups (500 mL) water

3 tbsp. (50 mL) coarse salt

2 tbsp. (30 mL) honey

2 tbsp. (30 mL) peppercorns

2 cinnamon sticks

1 handful of fresh dill (if possible) or
2 tbsp. (30 mL) dried dill

2 to 4-lb (1 - 2 kg) piece of fresh salmon

In a plastic or ceramic dish large enough to hold the fish, place all the ingredients except the salmon. Bring to boil 10 minutes at HIGH. Then, simmer covered, 10 minutes at MEDIUM. Put the salmon piece into the court-bouillon while it is still hot. Cover and cook 6 minutes per pound (500 g) at MEDIUM, turning the fish over after 6 minutes. Remove from oven. Baste the fish. Remove the cinnamon sticks. Cover and let it cool for 30 minutes before refrigerating it.
Let the fish marinate in its juice for 2 days before serving it. Serve as indicated above.

Scandinavian Marinated Salmon (photo page 48-49)

In the Scandinavian countries where salmon abounds in season, raw fish is cooked in a marinade mixture and can be kept, refrigerated and covered, in excellent condition for 2 to 3 weeks. Turn fish over in the marinating mixture once a week.

1/3 cup (80 mL) cider or white wine vinegar

2 cups (500 mL) of any type of white wine

1 large onion, thinly sliced

2 tbsp. (30 mL) coarse salt

1 carrot, peeled and thinly sliced

3 whole cloves

1 tbsp. (15 mL) dried dill or dill seeds or
6 to 10 sprigs of fresh dill

1 tsp. (5 mL) whole peppercorns

3 to 4 lb (1.5 to 2 kg) fresh salmon, whole
or sliced

Place all the ingredients, except the salmon, in a dish large enough to hold the whole fish. Cover and cook at HIGH 6 minutes. Add the fish. Roll around in the liquid. Cover and cook at MEDIUM 5 minutes per pound (500 g). The fish is cooked at MEDIUM because it must not boil.
Cool for 20 minutes, then refrigerate in its court-bouillon, well covered.
In Norway, where I learned to cook salmon in this manner, it is served cold, in a glass dish with some of the strained marinade poured on top. A dish of hot boiled new potatoes, a small bowl of minced dill and a bottle of Scandinavian mustard (Dijon type can replace it when it is hard to find Scandinavian type) are served with the salmon. Super delicious with a glass of aquavit.

Scottish Molded Salmon

An attractive and tasty way to use fresh or leftover poached salmon.

2 to 3 cups (500 mL to 750 mL)
   poached salmon
1 envelope of unflavored gelatine
1/4 cup (60 mL) scotch or white wine or water
2 tsp. (10 mL) prepared mayonnaise

1 tsp. (5 mL) curry powder
Capers
Lemon wedges
Shredded lettuce or watercress

Remove skin and bones from the fish. Measure the 2 to 3 cups (500 to 750 mL). Oil a nicely shaped mold of your choice and pack in the salmon. Cover and refrigerate for a few hours.
Sprinkle gelatine over the cold liquid of your choice. Cook 1 minute in the Microwave at MEDIUM. Meanwhile, pour into a bowl, the mayonnaise and curry powder. Add the gelatine to this mixture while beating constantly. Refrigerate 10 minutes, or until it is just partly set.
Unmold the fish on a service platter, spread generously with the jellied mayonnaise. Decorate the top with dots of capers. Place lemon wedges around, standing them against the fish. Surround with a thick layer of shredded lettuce or watercress.
Refrigerate until ready to serve.

Poached Salmon Hollandaise

An excellent recipe to cook a thick piece of fresh salmon, served cold with a French mustard Hollandaise.* Perfect for a buffet or an intimate garden party. Cook in the convection section of your Microwave oven.

2 lb (1 kg) center piece of salmon
1/3 cup (80 mL) melted butter
1/3 cup (80 mL) dry vermouth or fresh lemon
   juice

Salt and pepper to taste
3 sprigs of fresh basil or
   1 tsp. (5 mL) dry basil

Place the piece of salmon on a rack and set in a 9-inch (22.5 cm) pie plate. Melt the butter 1 minute at HIGH and pour over the fish. Then pour around it the vermouth or lemon juice. Salt and pepper to taste. Sprinkle with the basil. Bake in oven set at 350°F (180°C), 30 minutes or 10 minutes per inch (2.5 cm) thick. When cooked, remove from Microwave, cover dish with plastic wrap. Cool, then refrigerate for 12 hours. The juice turns into a delicious jelly that is served with the fish.
Also make Mustard Hollandaise, for each one to use to taste.

* See Sauce chapter.

Vancouver Salmon Loaf

Serve it hot with a herb or green pea white sauce, or cold with mayonnaise garnished with diced gherkins, finely chopped parsley and green onions.

1 15.5-oz (439 g) can salmon	1/2 tsp. (2 mL) curry powder
1 lightly beaten egg	1 small onion, grated
1 cup (250 mL) fresh breadcrumbs	1 tsp. (5 mL) salt
1/4 cup (60 mL) whipping or sour cream	1/4 tsp. (1 mL) pepper
2 tbsp. (30 mL) celery leaves, minced	Juice and grated rind of half a lemon

Empty the can of salmon into a bowl, crush the bones with a fork, flake the undrained fish, and mix together with a fork.
Add the remaining ingredients. Mix thoroughly and place in a 9 x 5-inch (22.5 x 12 cm) loaf pan. Cover with waxed paper. Cook 6 to 9 minutes at HIGH. Let stand 5 minutes. Unmold and serve.

Darvish Salmon

I have often wondered where the name of this simple family dish comes from. Whichever place, it is economical as you can serve 4 to 6 people with a can of salmon.

1 15.5-oz (439 g) can salmon	3 green onions, finely minced
3 tbsp. (50 mL) butter	Salt and pepper to taste
3 tbsp. (50 mL) cornstarch	1 full cup (250 mL) soda crackers, crushed fine
2 cups (500 mL) milk	3 tbsp. (50 mL) butter

Empty a can of salmon on a dish and flake with a fork. Divide into 2 portions.
Place the 3 tablespoons (50 mL) of butter in a dish, melt 2 minutes at HIGH. Remove from oven, stir in cornstarch. Mix well. Add milk and green onions, salt and pepper, stir well. Cook at HIGH 4 minutes, stir well. The sauce should be creamy. If necessary, cook 1 or 2 minutes more.
Butter an 8-or 9-inch (20 to 22 cm) glass casserole, place in it one portion of the salmon and top with 1 cup (250 mL) of the sauce. Sprinkle with half the crackers. Dot with 1 tablespoon (15 mL) butter.
Repeat layers. Dot with remaining butter. Sprinkle generously with paprika. Cover with waxed paper or a cover. Bake 8 or 10 minutes at MEDIUM-HIGH.

Scandinavian Marinated Salmon
(page 46)

Cold Salmon "Superbe"

A speciality of the Norwegian cuisine, cooked in parchment paper. It is traditional to serve it with a cucumber salad and steamed potatoes.

A 2-lb (1 kg) piece of salmon

1/3 cup (80 mL) melted butter

Juice of 1/2 a lemon

1/3 cup (80 mL) vodka or white vermouth

Salt and pepper to taste

A few branches of fresh dill

Take a square of parchment paper* large enough to wrap around the fish.
Place the paper in an 8 x 8-inch (20 x 20 cm) glass dish. Set the fish on it. Rub all over with the melted butter. Pull up the paper to form a sort of open bag. Add the lemon juice, the vodka or vermouth, salt and pepper to taste. If the dill is fresh, place 2 to 3 flowering tops on the fish. Close the bag by folding the paper together.
Cook 20 minutes at MEDIUM-HIGH. Let stand 20 minutes. Do not open the package. When cool, refrigerate 12 hours. The juice will form a sort of jelly.
Serve on a bed of lettuce. Surround with parsley alternating with thin slices of lemon and cucumber.

* Parchment is not easily available. If you cannot find any, use a double layer of waxed paper, since it can be used in the Microwave.

Salmon Mousse

You may use canned salmon if you are unable to find fresh salmon. This light and delicate mousse is the ideal dish on a warm day or for a buffet.

1 envelope unflavored gelatine

2 tbsp. (30 mL) fresh lemon juice

Grated rind of half a lemon

**2 French shallots or
4 green onions**

**1/2 cup (125 mL) boiling water* or white wine
or Sake**

1/2 cup (125 mL) mayonnaise

**1 tsp. (5 mL) tarragon or
1 tbsp. (15 mL) fresh minced dill
(if available)**

**1 15½-oz can (439 mL) pink salmon or
Sockeye**

1 cup (250 mL) whipping cream

In the food processor or the blender, place the gelatine, lemon juice, lemon rind, French shallots or green onions and the chosen liquid, water, wine or Sake. Mix together at high speed until the onions are minced. Add the mayonnaise, tarragon or fresh dill and the undrained salmon (if using canned salmon). Cover and mix again 1 minute. Whip cream, and add it, one third at a time, beating 20 seconds after each addition. Season to taste with salt and pepper.
Rinse a 4-cup (1 L) mold in cold water, pour in the mousse, cover and refrigerate 12 to 14 hours.
To unmold, dip mold 2 seconds in hot water and invert on a serving dish. Devilled eggs may be placed around the mousse as a garnish.

* If you wish to boil the water in the Microwave, heat it 8 minutes at HIGH.

Trout

Fisherman's Delight *(cover photo)*

If someone at your house has the good fortune to catch some fine small brook trout for you to cook, why not try the following recipe; this is my favorite way to cook them.

Fresh trout

Green onions

Melted butter

Fresh ground pepper

Paprika

Clean and wash the trout under cold water. Pat them dry with a paper towel. Place a green onion cut in half inside each fish, close the opening with a wooden pick. Place the trout in a large dish, one next to the other, alternating heads and tails. Wrap the heads and tails separately in narrow strips of aluminum foil to prevent drying. Melt a little butter to which you add pepper and paprika. Do not salt. Brush each fish on both sides with this butter. Cover (for best results, fresh trout must be poached, not fried). It is important to choose fish of almost equal weight, from 1½ to 2 pounds (approximately 2 kg). If they vary too much in size, some fish will overcook while others do not cook enough. Allow 3 minutes per pound (500 g) at MEDIUM. Check if done after 10 minutes and unwrap heads and tails. Place the fish in a serving dish. Add melted butter to the juice in the serving dish.

Potted Trout

Impossible to be in England in the spring and not eat their famous potted trout. It can be prepared with fresh or frozen trout. Very nice to serve as an "amuse-gueule", or around the swimming pool.

2 to 3 small trout, fresh or frozen

1/4 cup (60 mL) all-purpose flour

1 tbsp. (15 mL) butter

2 tbsp. (30 mL) vegetable oil

1/2 tsp. (2 mL) curry powder

Salt and pepper to taste

1 or 2 tbsp. (15 - 30 mL) butter

The grated rind of 1 lemon

If using frozen fish, thaw according to methods for Defrosting fish at the beginning of the book. Roll each trout in the flour. Melt butter in a 9-inch (22.5 cm) ceramic or glass pie plate, 1 minute at HIGH. Add the oil, stir in the curry powder and heat 1 minute at HIGH. Roll the trout in this mixture. Cook 5 minutes at HIGH. Turn fish and let stand 5 minutes. Cool until it can be handled, then carefully lift flesh from bones and place in a dish. Break up into small pieces with a fork. Divide into small ramequins, add to remaining butter in the plate 1 or 2 tablespoons (15 - 30 mL) of butter and the grated rind. Heat 40 seconds at HIGH. Divide the butter equally over each ramequin of fish. Cover and refrigerate at least 6 hours before serving.

Very nice served with hot French bread, garnished to each one's taste with the potted trout.

Stuffed Brook Trout

Fresh trout caught in cold brook water, in the early spring, what a delight! Should you not have trout, any small fish may be prepared in this manner.

1/4 cup (60 mL) butter

4 to 6 green onions, minced

1 to 2 cups (250 - 500 mL) fresh mushrooms, minced

1 tbsp. (15 mL) dill, dried or fresh

1 tbsp. (15 mL) Dijon mustard

1/4 tsp. (1 mL) pepper

1 tsp. (5 mL) salt

2 tbsp. (30 mL) sherry

6 fresh trout, 1/2 lb (250 g) each

2 tbsp. (30 mL) butter

3 tbsp. (50 mL) flour

1/2 cup (125 mL) cream

1/2 cup (125 mL) white wine or white vermouth

2 tbsp. (30 mL) butter

1/4 tsp. (1 mL) sugar

Mix together in a dish the 1/4 cup (60 mL) butter, green onions, mushrooms, dill, pepper, mustard, salt and sherry. Cover and cook 5 minutes at MEDIUM-HIGH, stirring once.

In another dish, melt the 2 tablespoons (30 mL) butter 1 minute at HIGH. Add the flour and cream, stir and cook 3 to 4 minutes at HIGH, stirring after 2 minutes of cooking. When the mixture is thick and creamy, add it to the mushroom mixture. Clean the fish and stuff them with the mushrooms.

Secure the openings with wooden picks, place the fish in a dish, one next to the other.

Heat the white wine or white vermouth, butter and sugar 2 minutes at HIGH. Pour over the fish, cover and cook 8 to 9 minutes at MEDIUM-HIGH, or until the fish flakes. Serve with lemon slices.

Broiled Trout

Any small whole fish can be cooked in this manner. In Belgium, where the recipe was created, they use the small whiting. We can achieve success with this recipe when done in a browning dish.

4 to 6 small trout or whiting

3 tbsp. (50 mL) milk

1/4 cup (60 mL) flour

1 cup (250 mL) fine dry breadcrumbs

3 tbsp. (50 mL) butter

1 small onion, chopped fine

1 French shallot or 3 green onions, peeled and chopped

1/4 cup (60 mL) white wine

1 tbsp. (15 mL) cider vinegar

Wash fish under cold running water. Wipe with paper towel. Place milk in plate and roll fish in it, then in flour and breadcrumbs. Preheat a browning dish, 7 minutes at HIGH. Add the butter without removing the dish from the oven. It will brown very quickly. Without delay, place fish, one next to the other. Press lightly on each one to create perfect contact between the dish and the fish. Cook 4 minutes at HIGH. Turn fish over with a spatula. Let stand 5 minutes without any heat. Then cook 2 minutes at MEDIUM. Remove fish to a hot platter.
To the butter remaining in the dish, add the onion and shallot or green onions. Stir well. Cook 2 minutes at HIGH. Add the white wine and the vinegar. Stir well. Cook 1 minute at HIGH. Pour over the fish and serve with steamed potatoes.

Poached Trout with Clam Dressing

If your husband brings you his prize catch of trout or any other small fish, this is a good way to prepare them because they will keep refrigerated for 3 to 5 days.

2 tbsp. (30 mL) vegetable oil

1 to 3 lb (500 g to 1.5 kg) fresh trout, whole or filleted

1 tsp. (5 mL) salt

1 tbsp. (15 mL) each, parsley and sage

Juice of 1 lemon

1 5-oz (142 g) can of baby clams

1/4 tsp. (1 mL) thyme

12 stuffed olives, sliced, to garnish

Pour the oil into an 8 x 12-inch (20 x 30 cm) glass or ceramic dish, and without overlapping the pieces, place the whole or filleted fish in the dish.
Sprinkle with salt, parsley and sage. Sprinkle lemon juice over all.
Drain the clams and pour the juice over the fish. Sprinkle with the thyme.
Cover dish with cover or waxed paper and cook at MEDIUM-HIGH 6 to 12 minutes, depending on whether you have thin fillets or whole fish.
Cool, then drain the juice carefully without disturbing the fish. Refrigerate the fish and the broth separately.
When ready to serve, mix together the reserved clams and sliced olives. Add just enough broth to make a light sauce and pour over the fish.

Note: Excellent served with long grain rice, using the leftover fish stock to cook the rice.

Venetian Trout

The combination of cucumber, fresh spinach and tarragon gives Venetian trout a very special and interesting flavor. In the summer, I replace the tarragon by an equal quantity of chervil.

4 medium or 6 small trout

1/2 cup (125 mL) white wine or fish fumet

1 tbsp. (15 mL) fresh lemon juice

1/4 cup (60 mL) water

1 small cucumber, peeled and diced

1 cup (250 mL) well-packed fresh spinach, chopped

1 tsp. (5 mL) tarragon or chervil

1 tbsp. (15 mL) butter

1½ tbsp. (15 mL) flour

2 egg yolks

1/4 cup (60 mL) butter

2 French shallots or 6 green onions, peeled and chopped

Clean the trout. Place them one next to the other in an 8 x 12-inch (20 x 30 cm) glass dish, add the wine or fish fumet, the lemon juice and water, salt and pepper to taste. Cover dish with waxed paper or a cover. Cook at MEDIUM-HIGH 10 to 12 minutes. When fish is cooked whole, turn with two forks after 3 minutes of cooking.

In the meantime, peel and dice the cucumber. Wash and chop the spinach. When using fresh herbs, chop them and measure them.

Melt the tablespoon (15 mL) of butter in a dish, 1 minute at HIGH. Remove from heat, add the flour, mix well. Set aside. Remove fish to a platter with a perforated spoon. Keep warm.

Pour the juice from the fish into the flour mixture. Beat in the egg yolks, add the cucumber and spinach. Stir well. Add shallots or green onions and cook 2 minutes at HIGH, stirring once. Remove from oven, add the remaining butter, a small piece at a time, beating well at each addition. Cook another minute at MEDIUM-HIGH, and pour over the fish.

Haddock

Fish Custard

A Scandinavian way to serve fillets of haddock or fillets of flounder.

4 fillets of haddock or flounder
1 tsp. (5 mL) lemon juice
2 tbsp. (30 mL) fresh dill, chopped

1 egg
1/2 cup (125 mL) milk

Brush each fillet lightly with lemon juice. Salt and pepper to taste. Roll up the fillets, hold with pick if necessary, spinkle with the dill. Place in a 9-inch (22.5 cm) pie plate or a small quiche dish. Beat egg and milk together and pour over the fish.
Cover and cook at MEDIUM 4 to 7 minutes, or until custard is set.

Haddock "À la grecque"

1 19-oz (540 mL) can undrained tomatoes
1/2 cup (125 mL) crumbled soda crackers
1 tsp. (5 mL) sugar
1/4 tsp. (1 mL) basil
1/2 tsp. (1 mL) salt
1 lb (500 g) frozen haddock

3 green onions, chopped fine
1/4 cup (60 mL) chopped parsley
1/4 cup (60 mL) vegetable oil
2 tbsp. (30 mL) flour
1 tbsp. (15 mL) paprika

Place the tomatoes and soda crackers in the bottom of an 8 x 8-inch (20 x 20 cm) glass dish. Sprinkle with basil, sugar and salt. Mix together with a fork. Set the frozen block of fish over the tomatoes. Mix together the remaining ingredients and pour over the fish.
Cover with waxed paper. Cook at HIGH 8 to 10 minutes, until the fish is well cooked in the center. Let stand 5 minutes. Serve.

Icelandic Poached Haddock

What makes this special is the coating of fresh parsley and dill. In the winter, when fresh dill is difficult to find, replace it by 1/2 teaspoon (2 mL) of dill seeds.

1½ to 2 lb (750 g to 1 kg) fresh or frozen fillets of haddock

4 cups (1 L) boiling water

3 medium-size onions

1 bay leaf

1 tbsp. (15 mL) fresh dill or 1/2 tsp. (2 mL) dill seeds

1/4 tsp. (1 mL) each of thyme and whole peppercorns

2 tbsp. (30 mL) butter

1 tbsp. (15 mL) flour

2 tbsp. (30 mL) fine dry breadcrumbs

1/4 cup (60 mL) finely chopped parsley (optional)

If fish is frozen, defrost. Cut thawed out or fresh fish into individual portions. Place in a dish large enough to hold the fish pieces one next to the other. Place in a bowl, the boiling water, onions, bay leaf, dill, thyme, peppercorns and 1 tablespoon (15 mL) of the butter. Cook 10 minutes at HIGH

Pour over the fish. Cover with waxed paper. Cook at HIGH 6 minutes per pound (500 g), or more or less, depending on type of fish used. Test with the point of a knife after 4 minutes of cooking, and cook 1, 2 or 3 minutes more.

This is necessary because you have a choice of fish, and some take slightly longer to cook than others. When fish is cooked, set aside in a warm place.

Melt the remaining butter. In another dish, mix in the flour, breadcrumbs and 1 cup (250 mL) of strained fish stock. Stir and cook 3 minutes at HIGH. Stir, and if necessary, cook another minute or 2 until sauce is lightly creamy.

Pour on top of fish and sprinkle with parsley.

Note: The leftover fish stock can be strained, frozen and used as liquid in any fish sauce, or to cook fish.

Butter Poached Haddock

Easy and quick to make. Fresh cod can replace the haddock. Do not let the simplicity of the sauce deceive you; it is colorful and very tasty.

1½ to 2 lb (750 g to 1 kg) fillet of haddock
1/3 cup (80 mL) butter
Salt and pepper to taste
Grated rind of 1 lemon

Juice of 1/2 a lemon
2 tbsp. (30 mL) fresh or dried dill
1 tbsp. (15 mL) fresh parsley, minced

Place the fish in a bowl. Cover with cold water and add 3 tablespoons (50 mL) coarse salt. Let soak for 1 to 2 hours. This is done to prevent the fish from drying while cooking.
Then, remove from the water, dry with paper towel.
Melt the butter 1 minute at HIGH in an 8 x 8-inch (20 x 20 cm) baking dish. Place the fillets, either cut in individual portions, or rolled or left whole, in a dish. Cover with plastic wrap or cover. Cook 6 minutes per pound (500 g) at HIGH. Let stand 3 minutes, covered. Then, remove from dish with a spatula or a perforated spoon. Place on a warm platter. Salt and pepper to taste.
To juice in the baking dish, add the lemon rind and juice, the dill and parsley. Heat 1 minute at HIGH. Pour over the fish and serve with boiled potatoes.

Haddock "À la Royale"

"À la Royale" is the name given to fish cooked in a piece of parchment or in a cooking bag.

4 medium haddock fillets
2 tbsp. (30 mL) melted butter
4 tbsp. (60 mL) flour
1 tsp. (5 mL) salt

1/2 tsp. (2 mL) pepper
1/2 tsp. (2 mL) paprika
1/2 cup (125 mL) mild cheese, grated
1/2 cup (125 mL) milk or cream

Cut the fillets into individual portions. Brush each piece with melted butter. Mix together the flour, salt, pepper and paprika. Roll each piece of fish in this mixture, then in the grated cheese. Place a cooking bag on a plate or in a 12 x 8-inch (30 x 20 cm) dish, and put the fish fillets into the bag one next to the other, add the milk gradually. Close the bag loosely and make two small incisions on top with the point of a knife. Cook 15 minutes at HIGH. When the fish is cooked, remove the fillets from the bag and place them on a serving dish. Sprinkle with minced parsley.
In the summer, I sprinkle the fish with fresh minced chives and I pour the sauce remaining in the bag over the fish.

Haddock "Printanier"

Often served in Scotland as a late Sunday breakfast with a basket of hot scones or biscuits, and a pot of very hot, very strong tea.

1½ lb (750 g) haddock steaks or fillets

4 tbsp. (60 mL) oil of your choice

3 garlic cloves

1 bay leaf

1 tbsp. (15 mL) flour

1/4 cup (60 mL) minced parsley

1/2 cup (125 mL) fish fumet or water

1 to 2 cups (250 to 500 mL) frozen green peas

Salt and pepper to taste

3 to 4 eggs

Wipe the steaks or fillets with absorbent paper.
In an 8 x 8-inch (20 x 20 cm) ceramic dish, heat the oil 3 minutes at HIGH. Add the garlic, bay leaf, flour and parsley. Stir thoroughly, add the fish fumet or water, stir well. Add the green peas. Cover with waxed paper. Cook 5 minutes at HIGH. Stir peas and juice. Let stand 4 to 5 minutes. Remove fish to a hot dish with a perforated spoon. Break the eggs into the juice. Pierce each yolk with the point of a paring knife. Cover with waxed paper and cook at MEDIUM, allowing 1 to 2 minutes per egg. As soon as the eggs are cooked, serve a portion of fish, an egg, and some gravy.

Baked Frozen Haddock Casserole

You will have an easily baked fish topped with a creamy tomato sauce. Serve with rice or mashed potatoes.

1 16-oz box (450 g) uncooked haddock fillets

Salt and pepper to taste

1 tsp. (5 mL) basil or
    1/4 tsp. (1 mL) curry powder

1 19-oz can (540 mL) tomatoes

2 tbsp. (30 mL) flour

1 onion, minced

2 celery stalks, chopped fine

1 tbsp. (15 mL) butter

1 egg, lightly beaten

1/4 cup (60 mL) cream

1 tsp. (5 mL) Worcestershire sauce

Season the thawed out fillets with salt and pepper to taste. Place them one next to the other in a 9 x 12-inch (22.5 x 30 cm) glass or ceramic dish.
Blend together the basil or curry powder, tomatoes, flour, onion, celery. Melt the butter 1 minute at HIGH. Add to mixture. Pour tomato mixture over fish. Cover dish with lid or waxed paper, and cook 10 minutes at MEDIUM-HIGH. Baste fish, and if necessary cook 1 or 2 minutes more at MEDIUM-HIGH. Remove fish from sauce, to a hot platter.
Beat the egg and cream together. Add the Worcestershire sauce and beat mixture into the fish tomato sauce. Cook 2 minutes at MEDIUM, stirring once after 1 minute. Pour over fish. Serve.

English Farmhouse Finnan Spaghetti

A true English family recipe and a pleasant change from the usual spaghetti sauce. The smoky taste of the haddock gives it an intriguing flavor.

1 lb (500 g) finnan haddock	3 tbsp. (50 mL) butter
1/4 tsp. (1 mL) summer savory	3 tbsp. (50 mL) flour
1 tbsp. (15 mL) vegetable oil	2 cups (500 mL) milk
1 tsp. (5 mL) salt	Salt and pepper to taste
8 oz (225 g) fine spaghetti	3/4 cup (190 mL) grated cheese
4 slices of bacon	1/4 tsp. (1 mL) nutmeg
1 large onion, thinly sliced	1 cup (250 mL) diced toasted bread

Bring 2 cups (500 mL) of water to a boil by heating 10 minutes at HIGH. Place the fish in a microwave safe dish, just large enough to hold it. Pour water over the fish, add the summer savory. Cover and cook 10 minutes at MEDIUM. Remove fish from water, let cool, then flake.

Place 2 cups (500 mL) of water in a 6-cup (1.5 L) bowl, bring to boil by heating 10 minutes at HIGH. Add the vegetable oil, salt and spaghetti. Stir well and cook 13 to 15 minutes at MEDIUM. Stir at half the cooking period. Spaghetti cooked in the Microwave is drained, but not rinsed. Dice the bacon, place in a dish, cook 2 minutes at HIGH. Stir well. Add the onion, stir and cook 2 minutes at HIGH. Add to the spaghetti with the flaked fish. Stir with a fork, blending gently.

In a 4-cup (1 L) measuring cup, make a white sauce by melting the butter 1 minute at HIGH. Add the flour. When well mixed, add the milk, stir and cook 3 minutes at HIGH. Stir well and cook another 2 to 3 minutes, or until creamy. Salt and pepper to taste, and stir in the nutmeg and grated cheese. Place the fish and spaghetti mixture in a bowl. Pour the cheese sauce over all. Cover with the diced toasted bread mixed with 1 teaspoon (5 mL) paprika.

When ready to serve, cover and warm up at "SENSOR I" or "COMB. I" if your oven has these features. The oven determines the time needed. Or, reheat at MEDIUM 3 to 5 minutes. Let stand 2 minutes.

American Haddock Casserole

Fresh or frozen cod can replace the haddock.

1 lb (500 g) haddock fillets

1/4 tsp. (1 mL) each salt and pepper

A pinch of nutmeg

1 can cream of mushroom soup

1/4 cup (60 mL) cream

1/4 cup (60 mL) milk or white wine

1/2 tsp. (2 mL) tarragon or thyme

1 cup (250 mL) Swiss or cheddar cheese, grated

Cut the fillets into individual portions. Place in an 8 x 8-inch (20 x 20 cm) dish, one next to the other, whole or rolled, with thicker pieces toward the edges of the dish. Mix together the salt, pepper and nutmeg. Sprinkle over the fish.

Mix together the cream of mushroom, cream, wine or milk and tarragon or thyme. Spread over fish. Sprinkle grated cheese over all. Cook 8 to 10 minutes at MEDIUM.

Finnan Haddock Pudding

A smoked or finnan haddock pudding is a light fluffy pudding. Serve with a green salad prepared with oil and wine vinegar.

1 lb (500 g) finnan haddock

2 slices of bacon, diced

1 tbsp. (15 mL) butter

2 cups (500 mL) mashed potatoes of your choice

Pepper to taste

Juice and grated rind of 1/2 a lemon

1 small onion, minced

1/2 tsp. (2 mL) celery salt

1/4 cup (60 mL) minced parsley

1/2 tsp. (2 mL) summer savory

3 tbsp. (50 mL) butter

3 eggs

Paprika

Place the fish in a 9-inch (22.5 cm) pie plate. Sprinkle bacon on top and add just enough water to cover bottom of dish. Cover and cook 10 minutes at MEDIUM. Remove fish to a hot plate and rub top of fish with the 1 tablespoon (15 mL) of butter. Cool.

Note: This is the basic way to cook finnan haddock.

When fish is cool, flake and add to the mashed potatoes. Add pepper, lemon juice and rind, onion, celery salt, parsley and savory. Beat together until thoroughly mixed. Melt the 3 tablespoons (50 mL) of butter 1 minute at HIGH. Add to the fish mixture. Separate the eggs, beat the yolks until light. Stir into fish and potato mixture. Beat the egg whites and fold gently into the mixture.

Butter a 4-cup (1 L) casserole and pour in the mixture. Sprinkle top generously with paprika. Bake 12 to 14 minutes at MEDIUM. Serve as soon as ready.

Cook
Cook Warm
Froz Cook
Froz Cook Warm

Cook (-Warm)
A1 : Reheat Pasta
A2 : Beef-Well Pork
A3 : Beef-Med
A4 : Beef-Rare
A5 : Stews
A6 : Potatoes Carrots
A7 : Vegetables-Soft
A8 : Fish Vegs-Firm

Froz-Cook (-Warm)
: Froz.Con.Foods(1-11oz)
: Froz.Con.Foods(12-22oz)
: Pot Roast
: Chicken Pieces
: Precooked Stews
: Hamburgers
: Vegetables
: Fish Fillets Scallops

Doneness Control   More   Less

Stop/ Reset   Clock   Start

Panasonic

Halibut "À la Russe"
(page 78)

Finnan Haddock

The smoked or finnan haddock is one of the world famous specialties of Scotland. It is possible all over Canada to find good smoked haddock. The following recipe is an authentic Scottish way of preparing it and I would like to add, the very best way.

1 lb (500 g) smoked haddock
2 tbsp. (30 mL) butter
1/4 tsp. (1 mL) pepper

1 cup (250 mL) milk or light cream
1 tbsp. (15 mL) cornstarch

Remove all skin from the fish, if necessary, and cut into serving size or bite size pieces. Melt butter in a 9-inch (22.5 cm) pie plate 2 minutes at HIGH. Add the fish, sprinkle with the pepper, cover. Cook at MEDIUM-HIGH 3 minutes.
Mix the milk or cream with the cornstarch. Pour over the fish. Simmer at MEDIUM-LOW 5 minutes. Stir and serve as soon as ready.
The traditional garnish is boiled peeled potatoes and finely chopped parsley.

Cod

Poached Cod "Fines-Herbes"

In spite of general opinion, fresh cod is delicious, and doubly so when poached in the Microwave. Frozen cod can be used, but it must be thawed before cooking.

2 lb (1 kg) fresh cod steaks or fillets

1¼ cups (310 mL) water or milk

1 medium onion, minced

1 bay leaf

3 slices of lemon, unpeeled

1 tsp. (5 mL) salt

4 peppercorns

2 tbsp. (30 mL) butter

2 tbsp. (30 mL) flour

1 tbsp. (15 mL) lemon juice

1/4 cup (60 mL) fresh parsley or
   2 tbsp. (30 mL) fresh dill

Set the fillets in one layer in an 8 x 12-inch (20 x 30 cm) glass dish. Pour the liquid over the fish. Cover with the onion and lemon slices, the bay leaf, salt and peppercorns. Cook, uncovered, 3 minutes at HIGH. Tilt the dish and pour the cooking juice over the fish with a spoon. Cook 4 minutes more at HIGH. Cover and let stand 3 minutes. Remove fish to a warm platter with a perforated spoon. Mix together the butter and flour, add to the fish juices, mix thoroughly. Add the lemon juice, parsley or dill. Mix well. Cook 2 minutes at HIGH. Stir. The sauce should be light and creamy; cook one minute more, if necessary. Pour over the fish.

Scandinavian Poached Cod

You may use this recipe to poach the same quantity of salmon. Small 6-ounce (175 g) fillets or steaks, either cod or salmon, are the easiest to poach.

1 cup (250 mL) hot water

Juice of 1 lemon

1 small onion, thinly sliced

1 celery stalk, diced

2 garlic cloves, crushed

1 bay leaf

1/4 tsp. (1 mL) thyme

4 whole cloves

1 tsp. (5 mL) salt

1/4 tsp. peppercorns

4 to 6 cod steaks or fillets, 6 oz (175 g) each

Place all the ingredients, except the cod, in a glass dish. Cover, cook 6 minutes at HIGH to bring to boil. Stir thoroughly, and place the fish pieces side by side. Cover and poach 2 minutes at HIGH. Turn each piece carefully, cover and poach 1 minute at HIGH. Let stand 5 to 8 minutes before serving. Serve with butter melted with a little lemon juice and chopped parsley, or with a parsleyed white sauce.

Poached Cod with Egg Sauce

Very interesting lunch, very New England in the spring. Delicious, served with small boiled new potatoes and fresh June green peas, both easy to do in the Microwave.*

2 lb (1 kg) cod steaks or fillets, fresh or frozen

1½ cup (375 mL) boiling salted water

1 tsp. (5 mL) thyme

1 medium-sized onion, thinly sliced

1 bay leaf

4 sprigs of parsley

1 celery stalk, quartered

Sauce:

1/4 cup (60 mL) butter or margarine

3 tbsp. (50 mL) flour

Drained fish cooking water

1/4 tsp. (1 mL) salt

1/4 cup (60 mL) light or heavy cream

1/4 cup (60 mL) minced parsley

2 to 3 hard cooked eggs, sliced

Place the steaks or fillets of cod in a glass or ceramic dish. Add enough boiling water to just come to edge of fish without covering it, then add thyme, onion, bay leaf, parsley and celery. Cover and cook 10 minutes at HIGH. Let stand 10 minutes.

To make sauce, melt the butter or margarine in a 4-cup (1 L) measuring cup, 1 minute at HIGH. Add the flour, mix well, add the fish cooking liquid and the salt. Stir well. Cook 4 minutes at MEDIUM-HIGH. Stir well, add the cream and the parsley and cook another 3 minutes at MEDIUM. Stir well, add the eggs. Salt and pepper to taste.

Drain the remaining water from the fish. Place on a warm dish and pour the sauce over all.

* *Note: You will find the recipe to cook the fresh green peas and the boiled new potatoes in the Vegetable book.*

Acadian Baked Cod with Vegetables

A summer meal in one dish, fish, tomatoes, green pepper and potatoes... tasty, colorful and economical.

About 2 lb (1 kg) fresh cod steak	1 onion, thinly sliced
Grated rind of 1 lemon	2 tomatoes, peeled and sliced
1/4 tsp. (1 mL) pepper	3 potatoes, peeled and sliced paper-thin
1 tsp. (5 mL) salt	1 green pepper, cut in slivers
1/4 tsp. (1 mL) thyme	2 tbsp. (30 mL) butter or margarine
Juice of 1/2 a lemon	3 tbsp. (50 mL) minced parsley

Mix the lemon rind, salt, pepper and thyme, rub all over the fish. Place in a 7 x 11-inch (17.5 x 27.5 cm) glass or micro-safe dish. Sprinkle with the lemon juice. Let stand 20 minutes. Remove fish from dish. Arrange half the onion, tomatoes, potatoes and green pepper in the dish. Top with fish and add the remaining vegetables.
Melt the butter or margarine 1 minute at HIGH. Add the parsley. Pour over the vegetable topping. Cover with waxed paper. Bake 8 to 10 minutes at HIGH, basting once with juice in the dish after 3 minutes. Let stand 3 minutes and serve.

Gratin of Cod and Celery

Red snapper is also very interesting prepared in this manner. The flavoring of dill and celery seeds and the topping of braised celery give it color and flavor.

1/2 tsp. (2 mL) dill seeds	*Braised Celery:*
1/4 tsp. (1 mL) celery seeds	1 tbsp. (15 mL) butter
1/4 tsp. (1 mL) pepper	4 celery stalks, sliced
1/2 tsp. (2 mL) salt	1 tbsp. (15 mL) water
1½ lb (750 mL) cod or snapper fillets	1 thick slice of lemon, unpeeled
2 tbsp. (30 mL) butter, melted	3 tbsp. (50 mL) chopped parsley
Paprika to taste	Salt and pepper to taste

Combine dill and celery seeds with salt and pepper. Sprinkle over the fish. Refrigerate, covered, for 1 hour.
Place fish fillets in an 8 x 12-inch (20 x 30 cm) buttered dish one next to the other, seeds-side up.
Melt the butter 1 minute at HIGH, pour over fish. Sprinkle the whole with paprika.
To prepare the celery, melt the butter in a dish 1 minute at HIGH. Add the celery, water and lemon slice. Cover and cook 3 minutes at HIGH. Stir well. Let stand 5 minutes. Stir in the parsley, salt and pepper to taste. Place around the fish. Cover and cook 6 to 8 minutes at HIGH, according to thickness of fillets. Serve with parsleyed noodles or rice.

Hungarian Cod Casserole

An unusual and interesting combination of fish, sour cream and potatoes.

3 medium potatoes

1 lb (500 g) cod or halibut steaks

Salt and pepper to taste

1½ cup (375 mL) thinly sliced onions

4 to 6 bacon slices

Juice and rind of a small lemon

2/3 cup (160 mL) commercial sour cream

1/4 cup (60 mL) commercial sour cream

1/2 tsp. (2 mL) paprika

Wash and scrub the potatoes, make 2 or 3 incisions in the peel with the point of a knife. Place the potatoes in a circle on a microwave rack. Cook 8 to 9 minutes at HIGH. Check doneness with the point of a knife. If necessary, cook 1 or 2 minutes more. When cooled, peel the potatoes, slice them and place them in an 8 x 8-inch (20 x 20 cm) well-buttered dish. Salt and pepper to taste. Place the onions in another dish, without fat, cook 3 minutes at HIGH, stirring after 2 minutes of cooking. Remove from Microwave. Place the bacon on two layers of paper towel, cook 3 or 4 minutes at HIGH or until crisp. Some bacon may require only 2 minutes of cooking. Place the fish steaks over the potatoes. Sprinkle with the lemon juice and the rind, then with the onions, and finally with the crumbled bacon. Cover it all with the 2/3 cup (160 mL) sour cream. Salt and pepper to taste.
Cover the dish and cook at HIGH approximately 8 minutes or until the fish flakes. Mix the remaining sour cream with the paprika. Spread over the cooked fish, cover and cook 1 more minute at HIGH.

Spring Breeze Cod *(first photo)*

An amazing combination of asparagus and cod. Both flavors blend very well.

1 lb (500 g) fresh asparagus

1/4 cup (60 mL) cold water

3 tbsp. (50 mL) unsalted butter or olive oil

2 medium garlic cloves, minced

1/4 cup (60 mL) fresh parsley, minced

1/2 tsp. (2 mL) tarragon

2 lb (1 kg) fresh cod, cut into 6 fillets

The rind and juice of half a lemon

3 tbsp. (50 mL) heavy cream

Snap off the tough lower portion of each stalk, it will break where the tender part begins. Wash the asparagus and place them in a dish. Add the cold water and a pinch of sugar. Cover and cook 5 to 7 minutes at HIGH, or until the asparagus are tender. Check doneness with the point of a knife.*
Remove the asparagus from its juice, setting it aside. Keep the asparagus warm. Place the butter or oil, garlic, parsley and tarragon in a baking dish. Cook 3 minutes at HIGH, stirring once. Top with the fish, add the lemon rind and juice and the asparagus cooking juice. Salt and pepper to taste. Cover. Cook 6 minutes at MEDIUM-HIGH. Place the asparagus over the fish, cover and cook 2 minutes at MEDIUM. Place the fish and asparagus in a warm serving dish. Add the cream to the juice in the cooking dish, cook 3 minutes at HIGH, stir well and pour over the fish.

* You may also cook asparagus by Sensor, if your oven has that feature. The oven determines the cooking time.

Kedgeree

An old English breakfast or light lunch, still very much in favor. An interesting way to use leftover poached salmon or canned salmon.

1/4 cup (60 mL) butter or margarine

1/2 cup (125 mL) onions, chopped fine

1 garlic clove, chopped fine

2 celery stalks, diced

1/4 cup (60 mL) minced celery leaves

1 tart apple, peeled, cored and chopped

1 to 2 tbsp. (15 to 30 mL) curry powder

1 cup (250 mL) long grain rice, cooked

2 cups (500 mL) chicken stock or water

1 tsp. (5 mL) salt

2/3 cup (160 mL) milk or cream

1 lb (500 g) cooked cod, haddock or salmon

Place the butter in an 8-cup (2 L) dish. Cook 2 minutes at HIGH. Add the onions, garlic, celery, celery leaves and apple. Stir well. Cook 5 minutes at HIGH. Add the curry powder, stir thoroughly. Then add the cooked rice, chicken stock or water, salt and milk or cream. Stir well. Cover. Cook 20 minutes at MEDIUM-HIGH, stirring after 10 minutes.

Let stand 15 minutes and stir in the fish of your choice. Serve. When prepared ahead of time, do not refrigerate, reheat 5 minutes at MEDIUM, covered, or use "COMB. I" indicating reheat; the oven then determines how long it will take to reheat. The dish must be well covered with plastic wrap, when using the "COMB.".

Halibut

Halibut "Orange"

Delicious served hot. Equally good, served cold. As halibut is available almost all year round, and is easily found frozen, I would like to recommend this fish dish for guests or when minutes are at a premium. I always keep a few boxes of frozen halibut in my freezer for emergencies.

2 lb (1 kg) fresh or frozen halibut	**1 tsp. (5 mL) lemon juice**
The grated rind of 1 orange	**Salt and pepper to taste**
The juice of 1 orange	**1/8 tsp. (.05 mL) nutmeg**
4 tbsp. (60 mL) butter	**1/4 cup (60 mL) minced parsley**

Thaw fish, if frozen halibut is used, 1 hour before cooking. When thawed out, wrap in paper towel to remove excess moisture. For fresh fillets, simply wrap in paper towel for a few minutes.
Place fish in a single layer in a large thickly buttered dish.
Combine remaining ingredients, except the minced parsley, and pour over the fish. Bake 10 to 12 minutes at HIGH, or until fish flakes when tested with a fork. Let stand 5 minutes, then remove to a hot dish. Pour on top any sauce remaining in the dish. Sprinkle with the minced parsley and serve.

Halibut "À la Grecque" *(photo page 16-17)*

In Greece, each portion of fish is wrapped in vine leaves. When I have the bottled type, that can be purchased in Greek shops, I use them. They can be replaced by leaves of Boston lettuce.

2 lb (1 kg) halibut fillets or steaks

1 head of Boston lettuce

1/4 cup (60 mL) minced parsley

1 bay leaf, broken up

1 small onion, diced

1/4 cup (60 mL) olive or vegetable oil

1/2 cup (125 mL) white wine or white vermouth

1 tsp. (5 mL) salt

1/4 tsp. (1 mL) cumin seeds

1 chicken broth cube

1 cup (250 mL) caper sauce*

Arrange a layer of lettuce leaves on the bottom of an 8 x 12-inch (20 x 30 cm) glass dish. Top with half the parsley, the bay leaf and onion slices. Sprinkle the remaining parsley on top. Place the halibut on top of this herb layer. Combine the oil, wine or vermouth, salt and cumin seeds. Pour over the fish. Break up the broth cube and scatter over the fish. Top with more lettuce leaves, enough to completely cover the fish.
Bake 10 minutes at HIGH, and 5 minutes at LOW. Let stand 5 minutes.
Set on a hot platter. Pour caper sauce on top and serve with rice, stirred with butter and minced parsley.
* See Sauce Chapter.

Halibut "À la Russe" *(photo page 64-65)*

Fresh or frozen fish can be used, the latter must be thawed before being prepared for cooking. Follow instructions on how to defrost fish (see index). This dish may be prepared a few hours ahead of time, refrigerated and cooked when ready to serve.

4 to 6 individual portions of halibut

1/2 tsp. (2 mL) each of salt and sugar

1/2 tsp. (2 mL) paprika

1 medium onion

6 thin slices of lemon, unpeeled

1 tbsp. (15 mL) butter

2 tbsp. (30 mL) chili sauce

Put the individual portions of fish in a round 8-inch (20 cm) dish. Mix together the salt, sugar and paprika. Sprinkle over the fish. Peel the onion and slice thinly, spread the onion ring over the fish. Top with the lemon slices.
Heat the butter and chili sauce 40 seconds at HIGH. Pour over the fish. Cover the dish with waxed paper. Cook 5 minutes at HIGH or 8 minutes at MEDIUM. Let stand 2 minutes before serving.

Halibut Stew

We seldom think of making a fish stew. However, if it is well prepared, a fish stew is a very economical and flavorful dish.

2 tbsp. (30 mL) butter
1 large onion, chopped fine
2 garlic cloves, chopped fine
1 small green pepper, diced
1 tomato, peeled and chopped
1 cup (250 mL) potatoes, peeled and chopped

1/2 cup (125 mL) water or clam juice
1 tsp. (5 mL) salt
1/2 tsp. (2 mL) pepper
1 tsp. (5 mL) dill or marjoram
4 to 6 halibut or cod fillets

Melt the butter 1 minute at HIGH, add the onion, garlic, green pepper and stir together. Cook 2 minutes at HIGH. Stir and add the remaining ingredients except the fish. Stir well, cook 5 minutes at MEDIUM-HIGH. Cut the fillets into individual portions and place them in the hot mixture, salt and pepper lightly. Cover and cook 5 minutes at HIGH. Let stand 3 minutes and serve with hot French bread.

Poached Halibut Rolls

Served in a nest of lemon rice, this is a deliciously light meal. Add a green salad, a fruit, and it is complete.

1½ lb (750 g) halibut or sole fillets
3 tbsp. (50 mL) butter
1/2 cup (125 mL) chicken broth or white wine
1 small garlic clove, minced
1/2 tsp. (2 mL) tarragon or basil

1 tsp. (5 mL) Dijon mustard
1 cup (250 mL) fresh tomatoes, minced
1/2 tsp. (2 mL) sugar
1/2 cup (125 mL) heavy cream
1/2 tsp. (2 mL) paprika

Wipe each fillet with a paper towel, cut in half lengthwise and roll up each piece. Melt the butter in a 9-inch (22.5 cm) round dish 1 minute at HIGH. Add the chicken broth or white wine, garlic, tarragon or basil, Dijon mustard, tomatoes and sugar. Cover and cook 5 minutes at HIGH. Stir well. Place the fish rolls side by side in the dish and baste with the sauce. Cook 8 minutes at MEDIUM-HIGH, basting with the juice halfway through the cooking. Remove the fish with a perforated spoon and place it in a warm dish. Cover. Add the cream and paprika to the sauce remaining in the cooking dish. Stir and cook 4 minutes at HIGH, stirring once. Pour over the fish and serve.

Boiled Lobster
(page 89)

Other delicious fish

Baked Pike with Sour Cream

Whenever I can purchase a 2 to 3-pound (1 to 1.5 kg) pike, and I have fresh dill in my garden, plus a good piece of cheddar, grated for this occasion, here is the recipe I use to best enjoy my baked pike. A small sea bass can replace the pike.

A 2-lb (1 kg) pike, cleaned but not split

1 tsp. (5 mL) salt

1/2 tsp. (2 mL) freshly ground pepper

1 cup (250 mL) sour cream

1/2 cup (125 mL) freshly grated cheddar cheese

1/4 cup (60 mL) fresh dill, minced

Paprika

Make 4 to 5 shallow gashes on both sides of the fish and season inside with salt and pepper. Make a paste with the sour cream, grated cheddar and dill, and spread this mixture on top and sides of the fish. Sprinkle generously with paprika. Place in a thickly buttered dish, long enough to hold the fish. Do not cover. Bake 6 to 8 minutes at MEDIUM-HIGH. The time will vary slightly, depending on the size of the fish. A good test is to lift a bit with a fork; if it flakes, it is cooked. When done, let stand 5 minutes, covered. To taste, sprinkle top with more minced dill.

Flounder Fillets Louisiana

When I have small fresh trout, I prepare them in the same manner. Flounder can also be replaced by fillets of sole, and canned salmon can replace the snow crabmeat.

1½ lb (750 g) fillets of flounder

1 tbsp. (15 mL) butter or margarine

3 tbsp. (50 mL) green onions, minced

3 tbsp. (50 mL) parsley, minced

1 medium sized onion, minced

1/2 lb (250 g) fresh crabmeat or
    1 8-oz (170 g) can snow crabmeat

1/4 cup (60 mL) fine cracker crumbs

1/4 tsp. (1 mL) curry powder

1/2 tsp. (2 mL) pepper and salt

1 egg white, lightly beaten

2 tbsp. (30 mL) cream or milk

Cut fish into 6 serving pieces, pat dry with paper towels. Place in a 7 x 11-inch (17.5 x 27.5 cm) glass baking dish.
Place butter or margarine in a dish, add the green onions, parsley and minced onion. Cook 2 minutes at HIGH. Stir well and cook at MEDIUM-HIGH another 2 minutes.
Stir in the crabmeat (use juice, when canned crab is used) and add the remaining ingredients. Stir the whole together.
Spread mixture over fillets in baking dish. Cover with waxed paper. Cook at HIGH 5 minutes or until fish flakes easily with a fork.
Garnish with parsley and lime or lemon slices.

Fillets of Flounder "Vin Blanc"

The flavoring combination of thyme and white wine is always perfect with all white fish.

1½ to 2 lb (750 g to 1 kg) fillets of flounder

2 tbsp. (30 mL) butter

1 10-oz (284 mL) can sliced mushrooms, drained

4 green onions, minced

Salt, pepper to taste

1 bay leaf

1/4 tsp. (1 mL) thyme

1/2 cup (125 mL) breadcrumbs

1/2 tsp. (2 mL) paprika

2 tbsp. (30 mL) butter, melted 1 minute at HIGH

1 cup (250 mL) white wine

Place fish in baking dish in rolled fillets or spread one next to the other. Melt the first 2 tablespoons (30 mL) of butter 1 minute at HIGH. Pour over fish. Mix the mushrooms, green onions, salt, pepper, bay leaf and thyme. Sprinkle over the fish.

Mix the breadcrumbs, melted butter and paprika, sprinkle over the fish, pour the white wine around it, not on top.

Bake at HIGH 6 to 8 minutes, basting with juice in dish, after 5 minutes of cooking.

Red Snapper Guadeloupe

The very first dish I ate on my arrival in Guadaloupe. I have often made it since. The lime, fresh mushrooms and parsley are very important. Also nice prepared with fillets of flounder.

2 lb (1 kg) red snapper fillets

1/4 cup (60 mL) butter or margarine

1/2 lb (500 g) fresh mushrooms, sliced

4 green onions, chopped

1/4 cup (60 mL) fresh parsley, minced

Juice of 1 lime or
    2 tbsp. (30 mL) lemon juice

1 garlic clove, crushed or chopped fine

1/2 tsp. (2 mL) salt

1/4 tsp. (1 mL) freshly ground pepper

Wipe fish with paper towel and place in an 8 x 8-inch (20 x 20 cm) glass or ceramic baking dish.

Melt the butter or margarine in a bowl 1 minute at HIGH.

Add mushrooms, green onions, parsley, lime or lemon juice, garlic, salt and pepper. Mix well. Cook 2 minutes at HIGH. Mix well, pour over fish spreading evenly. Cover with waxed paper. Cook at MEDIUM 6 to 7 minutes or until fish flakes easily. Serve with lime or lemon wedges for everyone to use at will.

Tuna and Macaroni Casserole

Vary the soup for different flavors.

2 cups (500 mL) elbow macaroni

1 tsp. (5 mL) salt

4 cups (1 L) boiling water

1 6½-oz (181 g) can flaked tuna

1 small onion, chopped fine

2 tbsp. (30 mL) chopped parsley

1/2 tsp. (2 mL) curry powder

1 10-oz (284 mL) can cream of chicken soup

1/2 cup (125 mL) buttered breadcrumbs

Place macaroni in an 8-cup (2 L) baking dish. Add salt and pour boiling water on top. Cook 8 to 10 minutes at HIGH. Stir thoroughly. Let stand 5 minutes, and drain.
Place all the ingredients except the buttered breadcrumbs in the baking dish and stir until well mixed. Add the macaroni. Mix well, top with buttered crumbs and dot with butter, cook uncovered 6 to 8 minutes at MEDIUM-HIGH. Let stand 5 minutes and serve.

Fish Casserole Creole

Use leftover fish or a frozen or fresh fish, poached, to make this tasty "meal-in-one dish".

1 to 1½ lb (500 to 750 g) cooked fish, broken into pieces

3 tbsp. (50 mL) butter

3 tbsp. (50 mL) flour

2 cups (500 mL) milk

1/4 tsp. (1 mL) dry mustard

Salt, pepper

1 tsp. (5 mL) sage or savory

1 10-oz (284 mL) can whole corn

2 eggs, separated

1/2 cup (125 mL) grated cheddar cheese

3 tbsp. (50 mL) soft breadcrumbs

1/2 tsp. (2 mL) paprika

Melt the butter 1 minute at HIGH in a large measuring cup. Add the flour, mix and add milk. Cook 3 minutes at HIGH. Stir well and cook another 2 minutes at HIGH or until creamy. Add mustard, salt, pepper to taste, sage or savory and corn. Stir, then cook another minute at HIGH. Add the egg yolks and 1/4 cup (60 mL) of the grated cheddar cheese. Mix thoroughly. Beat the egg whites until they hold a stiff peak, and fold into the sauce.
Butter an 8 x 8-inch (20 x 20 cm) glass or ceramic baking dish or a deep pie plate.
Fill with alternate layers of fish and sauce, ending with the sauce. Mix the remaining cheese with the breadcrumbs. Sprinkle on top of the sauce, and then sprinkle paprika over all. Cover with waxed paper. Bake 10 minutes at MEDIUM-HIGH.

Note: This casserole can be prepared early during the day, baking 10 minutes at MEDIUM-HIGH when ready to serve.

Seafood

Seafood Casserole *(last photo)*

A culinary delight from Nice, France, ready to serve in 8 minutes. Excellent fare for a friendly dinner, preceded by chicken consommé or cream of mushroom soup, with buttered rice and green peas as accompaniment.

2 tbsp. (30 mL) butter

1 tbsp. (15 mL) olive oil

A pinch of saffron or
    1/2 tsp. (2 mL) curry powder

1 tsp. (5 mL) paprika

1 medium onion, chopped fine

2 garlic cloves, chopped fine

2 tomatoes, peeled and quartered

1/2 tsp. (2 mL) sugar

1 green pepper, slivered

1/2 lb (250 g) medium shrimp, raw

1/2 to 3/4 lb (250 to 350 g) scallops

1/4 cup (60 mL) white wine or vermouth or
    fish fumet

Place the butter and olive oil in an 8 x 8-inch (20 x 20 cm) dish. Cook 3 minutes at HIGH. Add the saffron or curry powder, paprika, onion and garlic. Stir. Cook 1 minute at HIGH. Add the tomatoes, sugar and green pepper. Cook 1 minute at HIGH. Mix thoroughly.
Shell the shrimp and cut each scallop into 2 or 3 thin slices. Add to the tomatoes and stir well. Add the wine or vermouth or fish fumet. Cover the dish with waxed paper and cook 5 minutes at HIGH. Stir well and serve.

Boiled Lobster *(photo page 80-81)*

Steamed lobster, hot melted butter, crusty bread and a fine well chilled white wine. What more could one wish!

2 live lobsters, approximately 1½ lb (750 g) each

3 cups (750 mL) boiling water

2 bay leaves

3 slices of unpeeled lemon

The lobsters are cooked one after the other. Place the first one in a 12 x 8-inch (30 x 20 cm) dish and pour boiling water over it. Add bay leaves and lemon. Cover and cook 5 minutes at HIGH, turning the lobster twice. Remove from water. Cook the second lobster in the same manner. There is no need to change the water.
To serve, split the lobsters lengthwise, remove the sac and vein. Crack the claws. Serve on a warm platter with a small bowl of hot melted butter.

Lobster Newburg

This recipe may be used to garnish "vol-au-vent" shells, over toasted buttered French bread or simply served on a bed of parsleyed rice. Frozen tails must be thawed (see Index), and left to stand during preparation of the sauce.

1/4 cup (60 mL) butter

3 tbsp. (50 mL) flour

2 cups (500 mL) light cream

1 well-beaten egg

1 tsp. (5 mL) salt

2 tbsp. (30 mL) dry sherry

2 cans or 1 10-oz package of frozen lobster, or lobster tails, of your choice

Melt the butter 1 minute at HIGH in a 6-cup (1.5 L) baking dish. Add the flour and mix thoroughly. Add the cream and cook 3 to 4 minutes at HIGH, until thick and creamy, stirring twice. Add the egg gradually, beating with a whisk for perfect blending. Add salt and sherry, then the well-drained lobster, broken up into pieces, or the thawed lobster tail meat.
Heat the sauce, uncovered, 3 minutes at HIGH. Taste for seasoning and serve.

How to Cook Lobster Tails

Lobster tails are more economical to buy than whole lobsters, as proportionately there is more meat in the tails. Lobster tails are very easily cooked in the microwave oven.

2 lobster tails of approximately 8 oz (250 g) each

1/4 cup (60 mL) unsalted butter

2 tbsp. (30 mL) brandy, orange liqueur or lemon juice

Cut each tail lengthwise with kitchen shears. Brush the meat with melted butter. Place the lobster tails in a shallow dish, side by side. A good pinch of curry or tarragon may be added to the brandy or lemon juice, but not to the orange liqueur. Brush evenly over each lobster tail. Cover and cook 4 to 6 minutes at HIGH, according to size. When cooked, they will turn red.
Clarified Butter: Place 1/2 cup (125 mL) salted or unsalted butter in a cup, do not cover, cook 2 minute at HIGH. Cool, then with a small spoon remove the fat which has risen to the top. The milky residue remains in the bottom of the cup. Keep the clarified butter in the refrigerator until ready to use. Only 20 to 40 seconds at HIGH will be needed to reheat the butter. To taste, 1 teaspoon (5 mL) of orange liqueur, or scotch or lime or lemon juice may be added to the butter, before reheating.

Note: Do not discard the butter sediment. I use it in preparing soup, sauce or mincemeat.

Buttered Lobster Tails

The easiest recipe is often the most flavorful. To give it some style, serve it with imported chutney to which you add a few spoonfuls of brandy.

3 tbsp. (50 mL) butter

2 tsp. (10 mL) lemon or lime juice

1 10-oz (280 g) package of frozen lobster tails

Remove the tails from the package and place them in an 8-inch (20 cm) cake pan or in a 9-inch (22 cm) pie plate. Heat 2 minutes 30 seconds at HIGH without covering. Let stand approximately 5 to 10 minutes, covered, to thaw thoroughly.
Split the shells with kitchen shears by cutting the under part lengthwise. Press down to keep it flat. Set the tails side by side in an ovenware dish, meaty side up.
Melt the butter 1 minute at HIGH in a small bowl or a measuring cup, add the lemon juice. Stir to mix. Brush the lobster tails generously with this preparation. Cover and cook 2 minutes at HIGH, or just enough for the flesh to lose its transparency and turn pink.

Shrimp Vollarta *(photo page 96-97)*

This simple elegant dish calls for raw shrimp. Nowadays, this is a luxury! Choose the medium-sized shrimp. Most attractive served in shells.

1½ lb (750 g) fresh shrimp, medium-sized

The juice of 1 or 2 fresh limes

2 tsp. (10 mL) coarse salt

2 to 3 tbsp. (30 to 50 mL) vegetable oil

Split the shrimp in half lengthwise through the shell and tail. Rinse out dark vein. Dry shrimp on a paper towel, set on a pie plate and sprinkle the cut side of the shrimp generously with the lime juice. Salt and let stand a few hours in the refrigerator.
When ready to serve, heat the vegetable oil 2 minutes at HIGH, in a ceramic pie plate. Place about half the shrimp in the hot oil and cook until they turn pink, 3 minutes at HIGH. Cook the remaining shrimp in the same manner. Serve piping hot, surrounded with quartered limes.

Shrimp "Marinière"

Parisians are fond of this dish in the spring time. Fresh or frozen shrimp can be used.

1 10-oz (280 g) package uncooked frozen shrimp (shelled)

1/4 cup (60 mL) very hot water

2 tsp. (10 mL) lemon juice

1/4 tsp. (1 mL) salt

1/4 tsp. (1 mL) thyme or basil

1/3 cup (80 mL) dry white wine or vermouth

1/2 tsp. (2 mL) sugar

2 tbsp. (30 mL) oil

1 minced garlic clove

1 medium tomato, peeled and chopped

2 green onions, finely chopped

Place frozen shrimp in an 8-cup (2 L) glass baking dish. Defrost (see Index). Let stand 2 minutes. Separate the shrimp, and place them in a 4-cup (1 L) baking dish. Combine hot water, lemon juice, salt, basil or thyme, wine or vermouth and sugar. Pour over shrimp. Cook uncovered 4 minutes at HIGH. Let stand 1 minute. Drain and set aside. Pour oil into the 4-cup (1 L) baking dish, heat 1 minute at HIGH. Add garlic, tomato and green onions. Cook, covered with waxed paper, for 2 minutes at HIGH. Add shrimp, heat 2 minutes at HIGH. Serve with parsleyed rice.

Oriental Shrimp

Shrimp have become a great luxury, due to their cost, so I recommend that you use the green shrimp (raw), which are more tender and tastier. Serve with Rice Pilaf.

1 lb (500 g) shrimp, large or medium

3 tbsp. (50 mL) chili sauce

1 tsp. (5 mL) sugar

2 tsp. (10 mL) cornstarch

1/2 tsp. (5 mL) salt

1 tbsp. (15 mL) vegetable oil

2 tbsp. (30 mL) fresh ginger root, grated

1 garlic clove, crushed

1 small green pepper, slivered (optional)

1 tbsp. (15 mL) each soy sauce and sherry

Cut the shrimp like butterflies: A) Remove the shell by cutting with scissors all along the stomach and pull. B) Slit the stomach the length of the shrimp but without separating it in two. Flatten it out with your hands to shape it like a butterfly.

Mix together the chili sauce, sugar, cornstarch and salt. Place in an 8-inch (20 cm) round bowl, the oil, grated ginger and garlic.

Cover with waxed paper, and heat 2 minutes at HIGH. Remove garlic, add the green pepper and the chili sauce mixture, stir thoroughly, cover and cook 2 minutes at HIGH, stirring halfway through cooking. Add the shrimp, mix well, cover and cook 2 minutes at HIGH, stirring once halfway through cooking. Add soy sauce and sherry. Stir well and serve.

Shrimp "Provençale"

One of the great recipes of Provence!

Sauce:

2 French shallots or 6 green onions, chopped

1/2 cup (125 mL) white wine or white vermouth

1 bay leaf

1/4 tsp. (1 mL) thyme

1 tsp. (5 mL) basil

2 tbsp. (30 mL) butter

2 tbsp. (30 mL) flour

1 garlic clove, crushed or finely chopped

1 tsp. (5 mL) tomato paste

1/2 cup (125 mL) water, fish fumet or clam juice

1 lb (500 g) uncooked shrimp

1/2 cup (125 mL) water

1/2 cup (125 mL) button mushrooms, cut in four

2 medium sized tomatoes, diced

6 peppercorns

First, prepare the sauce. Place the shallots or green onions, white wine or vermouth, bay leaf, thyme and basil in a dish. Cook uncovered 3 minutes at HIGH. Mix together the butter and flour. Add to the wine sauce, stir well. Cook 2 to 3 minutes at HIGH, stirring once. Add the garlic, tomato paste and the liquid of your choice. Stir well and cook 4 minutes at MEDIUM-HIGH, stirring once.
Place the cleaned shrimp in a dish, add the water, mushrooms, tomatoes and peppercorns. Cook 3 minutes at MEDIUM-HIGH, stirring once. Remove peppercorns.
Pour the sauce over the shrimp or serve sauce separately. A nice way to serve these is to place the shrimp in a chafing dish and pass the sauce separately.

Shrimp in Hot Lime Butter

You may use lemon instead of lime. A quick and easy way to serve shrimp. They are at their best served hot.

1 6-oz (170 mL) bottle light beer

1/4 tsp. (1 mL) curry powder

1/2 tsp. (2 mL) paprika

1/2 tsp. (2 mL) dill seeds

1 onion, minced

1 lb (500 g) medium-sized shrimp

Melted or clarified butter to taste

The rind and juice of 1 lime or lemon

Pour the light beer into a large bowl, add the curry, paprika, dill and onion. Bring to boil 4 minutes at HIGH. Stir well. Add the shrimp. Stir, cover and cook 2 minutes at HIGH. Let stand covered 5 minutes. Remove the shrimp to a warm dish with a perforated spoon. Add the lime or lemon juice and the rind to the melted or clarified butter and serve with the shrimp. Peel off the shell and dip each shrimp in the hot lime butter.

Shrimp Victoria

A dish created for Queen Victoria to celebrate her fiftieth birthday. It is easy and quick to prepare and delicious to eat. Scallops or fresh oysters can replace the shrimp.

1 lb (500 g) medium-sized green shrimp or
  1 lb (500 g) fresh scallops
6 green onions, chopped fine
1/4 cup (60 mL) butter
1 tsp. (5 mL) curry powder
1/2 lb (250 g) fresh mushrooms, thinly sliced

2 tbsp. (30 mL) flour
1/4 cup (60 mL) dry sherry
1¼ cups (315 mL) sour cream
Salt, pepper to taste

Peel the green shrimp and shape them as butterflies by cutting inside the curve but without detaching. If you are using scallops, split in half on the thickness.

Place in an 8-inch (20 cm) round dish, the butter and green onions. Cook 1 minute at HIGH. Add the curry powder, stir until well mixed, add the mushrooms. Cook 3 minutes at HIGH. Stir well. Stir in the flour until well blended, add the sherry and stir. Cook 2 minutes at MEDIUM-HIGH. Stir thoroughly and set aside until ready to serve, as this portion of the recipe may be prepared 1 to 2 hours ahead of time. Do not refrigerate.

To reheat, cook 2 minutes at MEDIUM-HIGH, stir well, add the sour cream, stir to mix and heat at MEDIUM 3 to 4 minutes, or until hot. Serve in a nest of long grain rice stirred with lots of chopped parsley.

Hockey Night Seafood

Here is another fine fish stew served in a soup bowl, with a basket of large hot buttered biscuits.

1/4 cup (60 mL) butter or margarine
2 medium potatoes, diced
1/2 cup (125 mL) carrots, diced or minced
1 large onion, diced
1/4 cup (60 mL) water
1 lb (500 g) fresh or frozen haddock
2 5-oz (142 g) cans clams, drained

1 lb (500 g) scallops, cut in half
1 lb (500 g) small shrimp (optional)
1 cup (250 mL) light cream
Juice from the clams
1/2 tsp. (2 mL) curry powder (optional)
Salt and pepper to taste

Melt the butter or margarine 1 minute at HIGH, in an 8-cup (2 L) bowl. Add the potatoes, carrots and onion. Stir, add the water, cover and cook 10 minutes at MEDIUM-HIGH, stirring once after 5 minutes of cooking. Cut the haddock into small individual portions, add it to the vegetables together with the clams, and their juice. Cook 6 minutes at MEDIUM. Add the remaining ingredients. Stir well. When ready to serve, cover and cook 8 minutes at MEDIUM.

Scallops Saint-Jacques

A delectable dish of scallops, served either in a shell or in a nest of rice and topped with fresh minced parsley.

1 lb (500 g) fresh scallops

2 tbsp. (30 mL) butter

1/4 cup (60 mL) green onions, chopped

2 tbsp. (30 mL) flour

3/4 cup (190 mL) white or red wine

1/4 cup (60 mL) rich cream

1 small tomato, peeled, seeded and chopped

1/4 tsp. (1 mL) sugar

Salt and pepper to taste

2 tbsp. (30 mL) finely chopped parsley

When using big scallops, cut them in half to make two round slices. Leave the small ones whole. Melt the butter in an 8 x 8-inch (20 x 20 cm) glass or microwave-safe plastic dish, 2 minutes at HIGH. Roll the scallops in absorbent paper. Add to the butter. Cook at HIGH, 2 minutes. Stir well. Remove scallops from butter with a perforated spoon, cover and let stand. To the butter remaining in the pan, add the green onions, stir well, cook 2 minutes at HIGH. Add the flour, stir until well mixed, add the wine and the cream. Stir to mix. Add the chopped tomato and the sugar. Salt and pepper to taste. Stir the whole, cook 3 to 4 minutes at HIGH, stirring twice and cooking until creamy. Taste for seasoning. Add the scallops. Let stand, covered, until ready to use. To serve, either fill each shell to taste, sprinkle with parsley, place shells in the oven, on a sheet of absorbent paper, warm up, counting 1/2 minute per shell, or place in a ring of rice, sprinkle parsley over the whole, cover and warm up 3 minutes at MEDIUM-HIGH.

London Delight

Strolling along in London (England) one day, my eyes caught sight of a superb fish display. I stopped and looked with admiration. The owner came out, we talked, and he invited me to see how he cooked his scallops. Super!

1 lb (500 g) fresh scallops

6 to 10 slices of bacon

Chutney

Fresh lime, quartered (optional)

Pat the scallops dry in paper towels, then place them side by side in the bottom of a shallow pan, fit a microwave safe open low rack on top of scallops. Place slices of bacon on rack, one next to the other. Cook at MEDIUM-HIGH 6 to 8 minutes or until bacon is crisp. Remove bacon and keep warm. Remove grill. Stir scallops. Cook 3 to 4 minutes at MEDIUM-HIGH. Drain from fat. Add to bacon. Sprinkle with chopped parsley. Serve with toast or fine cooked noodles tossed with parsley or buttered rice.

How to Open Oysters and Clams

Many people find it difficult to open oysters and clams.
Your microwave oven will make it easy for you. Rinse the shells quickly under cold water, one at a time, as they should not soak. When rinsed, place the oysters or clams on a piece of newspaper (newspaper absorbs excess water) and cover them with paper towels. To open: place four or six oysters or clams in a circle on a double layer of paper towels in the microwave oven. Cook at HIGH 10 to 15 seconds. If the oysters are very large or very cold, it may take 16 to 17 seconds. Remove from oven as soon as you notice a fine split between the shells, it is then easy to open them with an oyster knife.

Nova Scotia Clam Chowder

A real treat from Eastern Canada. Well prepared, this is an interesting dish. Serve with hot biscuits or oatmeal bread. The clam chowder is served in a soup bowl although, strictly speaking, it is not a soup.

4 slices bacon, cut into small pieces

1 tbsp. (15 mL) butter or margarine

1 large onion, minced

1 cup (250 mL) potatoes, peeled and minced

2 cups (500 mL) hot water

20 oz (590 mL) fresh clams or undrained canned clams

2 cups (500 mL) light cream

Salt and pepper to taste

Place the bacon slices between two sheets of white towelling and cook 2 minutes at HIGH. Set aside. Melt the butter or margarine in an 8-cup (2 L) bowl, add the onion and cook 10 minutes at HIGH, stirring twice. Add the potatoes and water. Cover and cook at HIGH 4 to 6 minutes, or until the potatoes are cooked. Add the clams and their liquid together with the cream. Salt and pepper to taste. Stir thoroughly. Cook at HIGH 6 to 8 minutes, or until the chowder is hot. Garnish each bowl with the bacon pieces.

Shrimp Vollarta
(page 91)

Crab Quiche

I first ate this beautiful crustless quiche in Covey Cove, Nova Scotia. It can be made with canned or fresh crab or lobster. It was served with a fine-shredded cole slaw mixed with slivers of green and red peppers, lots of parsley and French dressing.

1 cup (250 mL) fresh mushrooms, thinly sliced

1 cup (250 mL) canned crab or lobster

2 tbsp. (30 mL) brandy or fresh lemon juice

1 cup (250 mL) grated cheddar or Swiss cheese

2 eggs

1 tsp. (5 mL) curry powder or tarragon

1 tbsp. (15 mL) flour

1/2 tsp. (2 mL) salt

1 cup (250 mL) light cream

Butter generously an 8-inch (20 cm) pie plate. Spread the mushrooms in the bottom. Shred the lobster or crabmeat, remove the bones, stir with the brandy or fresh lemon juice. Spread over the mushrooms. Top with the grated cheese.

Stir together until well mixed, the eggs, curry powder or tarragon, flour, salt and cream. Beat until well blended. Pour over the crab and mushrooms.

When ready to serve, cook 10 minutes at MEDIUM-HIGH. Let stand 5 minutes. If the custard is not sufficiently set, heat another 2 to 3 minutes at MEDIUM. Serve hot or cold.

Lemon Rice

Rice and fish always go very well together. You may, if you wish, prepare Lemon Rice ahead of time in a microwave-safe dish and reheat it, covered, 5 minutes at MEDIUM-HIGH, just before serving.

1 cup (250 mL) short grain rice

1½ cups (375 mL) water

1/2 tsp. (2 mL) salt

1/2 cup (125 mL) lemon juice

The rind of 1 lemon

3 tbsp. (50 mL) butter

2 - 3 tbsp. (30 - 50 mL) minced parsley

Place the water, salt and lemon juice in an 8-cup (2 L) dish. Bring to boil 5 minutes at HIGH. Add the rice, stir well, cover and cook 10 minutes at MEDIUM-HIGH. Stir well, let stand 15 minutes, covered. Cut the lemon rind into slivers. Place the butter in a dish, add the lemon slivers and juice, and the parsley. Cook 2 minutes at HIGH. Add this mixture to the cooked rice, stirring with a fork. Reheat 1 minute at HIGH, if necessary. Season to taste.

Sauces

Sauce Velouté

A basic white sauce, made with fish stock or canned clam juice or milk or light cream. It has many delicious variations.

2 tbsp. (30 mL) butter
2 tbsp. (30 mL) flour
1 cup (250 mL) fish stock or milk
Salt, pepper to taste

Place the butter and flour in a 4-cup (1 L) measuring cup, stir well. Cook 4 minutes at HIGH, stir after 2 minutes. The mixture will have little spots of brown here and there. This is as it should be. Add the fish stock or the juices from a poached fish or the milk. Salt and pepper. Cook 4 to 5 minutes at HIGH, stirring once. The Velouté has the consistency of a light white sauce.

Sauce Aurore
Variation of the Velouté

Excellent with salmon, cod and halibut.

1 cup (250 mL) Velouté Sauce
1/2 cup (125 mL) tomato sauce*

1/2 cup (125 mL) light cream
2 egg yolks, lightly beaten

In a 4-cup (1 L) measure, combine the ingredients. Stir until well mixed. Cook a MEDIUM, 4 to 5 minutes or until creamy, stirring once. The sauce should be light and creamy.

* Use the small can (11 oz - 213 mL) of tomato sauce, in the required quantity.

Lemon Sauce Velouté

Another variaton on "Velouté Sauce". Excellent with poached salmon or fresh thin cod fillets poached in milk.

2 tbsp. (30 mL) butter

2 tbsp. (30 mL) flour

1/2 tsp. (2 mL) salt

1 cup (250 mL) fish or chicken stock

2 egg yolks

1/2 cup (125 mL) light cream

3 tbsp. (50 mL) fresh lemon juice

The grated rind of half a lemon

In a 4-cup (1 L) measuring cup, stir together the butter and flour. Add the salt and fish or chicken stock. Cook 1 minute at HIGH, stir well and cook 2 minutes at MEDIUM-HIGH. Stir well, it should be creamy and smooth.
In a large bowl, beat the egg yolks and cream until smooth. Add the fish stock sauce, mix well, cook at MEDIUM 2 minutes. Stir again, add the lemon rind and juice, and cook another 1 or 2 minutes, beating once during the cooking period. Season to taste.
When you need to reheat, use MEDIUM heat for 1 or 2 minutes, stirring once.

Hollandaise Sauce and its Variations

A classic hot sauce, so easy to make in the microwave oven. I usually prepare everything and cook it when I am ready to serve it.

1/3 to 1/2 cup (80 to 125 mL) butter

2 egg yolks, lightly beaten with a fork

4 tsp. (20 mL) lemon juice

Salt, pepper to taste

Place the butter in a 2-cup (500 mL) measure. Cook at HIGH 2 minutes. Add the egg yolks and the lemon juice. Beat with a whisk until well blended. Cook at MEDIUM-HIGH 30 seconds, beat and cook again another 30 seconds, or until creamy. If the eggs are very cold, this can add another 10 seconds to the cooking. Salt and pepper to taste.

Hollandaise in Food Processor or Blender

Amazingly easy to prepare when done in the Microwave and food processor or the blender.

3/4 cup (190 mL) butter, cut up in squares

2 egg yolks

1 tbsp. (15 mL) fresh lemon juice

Salt, pepper to taste

Place the butter in a 2-cup (500 mL) measuring cup. Cook 3 minutes at HIGH.
Place the egg yolks and the lemon juice in the blender or food processor, cover and start the machine, slowly pour in the hot butter. When all is added, turn off the motor. Season to taste.

Dijon Hollandaise

Especially good served with hot or cold salmon or poached cod. The sauce can be hot or cold. Replace the lemon juice in the Hollandaise sauce by 2 tablespoons (30 mL) cold water mixed with a heaping tablespoon (15 mL) of Dijon mustard.

Blender Mustard Hollandaise

One minute in a blender to mix the ingredients and there you have a super Hollandaise to serve with fish.

4 egg yolks

2 tbsp. (30 mL) fresh lemon juice

1 cup (250 mL) butter

4 tsp. (20 mL) hot water

1/2 tsp. (2 mL) salt

1 tbsp. (15 mL) Dijon mustard

Combine the egg yolks and the lemon juice in the blender. Cover, blend 10 seconds. Melt butter 2 minutes at HIGH.
Gradually add hot water to egg yolks, while blending at medium speed, then add the hot butter, in a slow steady stream. Stop blender. Add the salt and mustard. Beat 20 seconds. Pour into warm dish and serve.

Mock Hollandaise Sauce

Not as rich as the true Hollandaise. Excellent to serve with cod, halibut or other types of white fish. I like to roll the cooked fish in minced parsley or chives, then top it with the Mock Hollandaise.

2 tbsp. (30 mL) butter

2 tbsp. (30 mL) flour

1/2 tsp. (2 mL) salt

1 cup (250 mL) milk

2 egg yolks, lightly beaten

2 tbsp. (30 mL) fresh lemon juice

The grated rind of 1/2 a lemon

2 tbsp. (30 mL) margarine or butter

In a 4-cup (1 L) measuring cup, melt the butter 1 minute at HIGH. Add the flour, mix well, add the salt and the milk. Stir and cook 3 minutes at HIGH, stirring once after 2 minutes of cooking.
When sauce is creamy, stir in the egg yolks, beat until well blended. Add the lemon juice and rind. Mix well, cook 1 minute at HIGH, beat and cook another 30 seconds.
Add the margarine or butter, salt and pepper to taste. Stir until the butter is melted. Serve.

Béarnaise Sauce

A Béarnaise is a variation of the Hollandaise. It is flavored with tarragon, white wine or cider vinegar, and a touch of green onion. At its best when served with hot seafood or hot salmon.

3 tbsp. (50 mL) cider or white wine vinegar

1 tsp. (5 mL) tarragon

1 green onion, chopped fine

4 whole peppercorns, coarsely crushed

1/3 cup (80 mL) butter

2 egg yolks, lightly beatean

Place in a 2-cup measuring cup (500 mL), the vinegar, tarragon and green onion. Cook 2 minutes at HIGH. Pass through a fine sieve, add the crushed peppercorns and the butter to the strained liquid. Cook 1 minute at HIGH.
Add the egg yolks, beat until well blended, cook 30 seconds at HIGH. Stir well and cook 20 to 30 seconds at HIGH, or until creamy, stir well and serve.

Sauce Bercy

When, after cooking a fish, you have 1 cup (250 mL) of liquid remaining in the pan and you wish to have an elegant sauce, I recommend "Sauce Bercy".

2 tbsp. (30 mL) butter

4 green onions, chopped fine

2 tbsp. (30 mL) margarine or butter

2 tbsp. (30 mL) flour

1/2 tsp. (2 mL) salt

1 cup (250 mL) fish cooking liquid

2 tbsp. (30 mL) fresh parsley, minced

Place in a dish the first 2 tablespoons (30 mL) butter and the green onions. Cook 2 minutes at HIGH. In a 4-cup (1 L) measuring cup, stir together the margarine or butter and the flour, add the salt and the fish cooking liquid.
Cook 1 minute at HIGH. Stir well and cook 2 minutes at MEDIUM-HIGH. Stir thoroughly, it should then be smooth and creamy. Add the parsley, stir well. Pour over the fish or serve separately.

Onion-Sage Fish Sauce

I make this sauce in the summer when fresh sage is plentiful in my garden and at the market. This sauce is good with all fish except sole.

1 tbsp. (15 mL) butter

1 large onion, minced

Salt and pepper to taste

1/2 tsp. (2 mL) dried sage or
   1 tsp. (5 mL) fresh sage, minced

1/2 cup (125 mL) light cream

1/4 cup (60 mL) water

2 tbsp. (30 mL) breadcrumbs

Melt the butter in a bowl 1 minute at HIGH. Add the onion, stir well and cook 3 minutes at MEDIUM-HIGH, stirring once. Salt and pepper to taste. Add the sage. Mix well and add the cream, water and breadcrumbs. Stir well. Cook 5 minutes at MEDIUM, stirring once during the cooking. The sauce should be thick and creamy. Season to taste.

Sea Island Curry Sauce

An intriguing sauce flavored with curry, and textured with coconut. When possible, use fresh coconut, grated, and use 1/2 cup (125 mL) of the coconut milk to replace 1/2 cup (125 mL) of the milk. Good on all poached or grilled fish.

1/2 cup (125 mL) grated coconut, fresh
   or dried

1 cup (250 mL) milk

4 tbsp. (60 mL) butter

2 onions, chopped fine

1 unpeeled apple, cored

2 small tomatoes, peeled and seeded

1 tbsp. (15 mL) curry powder

1 cup (250 mL) white wine

Place the coconut and milk in a bowl. Soak 30 minutes. Melt the butter in a bowl, 3 minutes at HIGH. Add the onions, stir and cook 2 minutes at HIGH. Stir, add the apple, tomatoes, curry powder and salt to taste. Stir thoroughly. Cook 5 minutes at MEDIUM-HIGH. Stir, add the coconut and milk and the white wine. Mix and cook 3 minutes at HIGH. Pass through a food mill or food processor. Taste for seasoning. Warm up 3 minutes at HIGH. Serve.

Oriental Sauce

Interesting and different, easy to make. Serve on any poached or steamed fish of your choice. Whenever possible use Sake as called for in the recipe. If not available, replace by white dry vermouth.

2 tbsp. (30 mL) cornstarch

1 cup (250 mL) pineapple or apple juice

1/4 cup (60 mL) Sake or white vermouth

2 tbsp. (30 mL) soy sauce

1 tbsp. (15 mL) dark brown sugar

1/4 cup (60 mL) cider vinegar

1 tbsp. (15 mL) grated fresh ginger root

Mix the cornstarch with 1/4 cup (60 mL) of the pineapple or apple juice.
Place in a large cup the Sake or white vermouth, the rest of the pineapple or apple juice, soy sauce, brown sugar, cider vinegar. Cook 5 minutes at HIGH, stir well. Add the well-stirred cornstarch and the fresh grated ginger. Cook 4 minutes at HIGH, stir well until creamy and transparent. Taste for seasoning, add salt if necessary. Pour over cooked fish.

Sauce Verte

If you have a food processor or a blender, this sauce will be ready in minutes. If not, the ingredients will have to be chopped very finely. It is an uncooked sauce, equally good served with hot or cold cooked fish.

1/2 cup (125 mL) green onion tops or chives

1/2 cup (125 mL) parsley

1/2 cup (125 mL) uncooked spinach leaves

2 tbsp. (30 mL) fresh lemon juice

1 cup (250 mL) mayonnaise

Coarsely chop the green onions or chives, the parsley and spinach. Place in food processor or blender, add the lemon juice and process until everything is in small bits. Add to mayonnaise. Stir well. Keep refrigerated, well covered.

Watercress Mayonnaise

An uncooked sauce, prepared in the food processor. Its deep green color is most appetizing.

1 bunch watercress, stems and leaves*

1/4 cup (60 mL) dill weed, fresh if available

4 green onions, coarsely chopped

1 tbsp. (15 mL) fresh lemon juice

1 cup (250 mL) mayonnaise**

Place all the ingredients in the food processor, cover and beat until the whole is creamy with a beautiful green color. Refrigerate until ready to serve. Taste for seasoning.

* About 2 to 3 full cups.
** Do not use a sweet mayonnaise.

Fish Marinade

The flavor of fish, fresh or frozen, pieces of salmon or cod, etc., is often enhanced if the fish is marinated before cooking. I also advise marinating fish which is to be served cold.

1/4 cup (60 mL) fresh lemon juice	**1 small onion, diced**
1/4 cup (60 mL) fresh lime juice (optional)	**1/2 tsp. (2 mL) each dill, tarragon and sugar**
1/4 cup (60 mL) olive or vegetable oil	

Mix all the ingredients together, pour over a piece of fish of 2 to 3 pounds (1 to 1.5 kg). Cover and refrigerate from 6 to 12 hours.

To cook the fish, remove from marinade, wipe dry with paper towel, and cook according to the chosen recipe.

Index

Give the **Encyclopedia of Microwave Cooking** to a friend!

Éditions Héritage
300, Arran, Saint-Lambert, Quebec
J4R 1K5

Send to:

*NAME:*_____

*STREET:*_____

*PROVINCE:*_____ *POSTAL CODE:*_____

___ copy(ies) of: **Meats and Sauces $14.95**

___ copy(ies) of: **Soups and Garnishes $14.95**

___ copy(ies) of: **Fish and Sauces $14.95**

___ copy(ies) of: **Poultry, Stuffing and Sauces $14.95**

Enclosed is $ per book plus $1.00 each for postage and handling. Total amount enclosed:
$_____
Make cheque or money order payable to Éditions Héritage. Prices subject to change without notice.

✂

Give the **Encyclopedia of Microwave Cooking** to a friend!

Éditions Héritage
300, Arran, Saint-Lambert, Quebec
J4R 1K5

Send to:

*NAME:*_____

*STREET:*_____

*PROVINCE:*_____ *POSTAL CODE :*_____

___ copy(ies) of: **Meats and Sauces $14.95**

___ copy(ies) of: **Soups and Garnishes $14.95**

___ copy(ies) of: **Fish and Sauces $14.95**

___ copy(ies) of: **Poultry, Stuffing and Sauces $14.95**

Enclosed is $ per book plus $1.00 each for postage and handling. Total amount enclosed:
$_____
Make cheque or money order payable to Éditions Héritage. Prices subject to change without notice.

Printed by
PAYETTE & SIMMS, INC.
in October, 1985
at Saint-Lambert, Qué.

Seafood Casserole
(page 89)